Learning Made Easy

PUNCTUATION
MADE
EASY

Publications International, Ltd.

Jeri Cipriano, M.A., has been creating classroom materials for more than 25 years and has written more than 50 books and countless magazine articles, games, and teaching materials for students in grades K–12. She served as Executive Editor for Newbridge Educational Publishing and Editorial Director for Scholastic, Inc.'s Magazine Division in reading and language arts.

Consultant:
Creative Services Associates, Inc., is a group of educators who have provided publishers with educational materials for more than 15 years.

Cover illustration: Garry Colby
Illustrations: Garry Colby, Rémy Simard

CONTENTS

Getting Your Directions Right

When you take a car trip, you follow street signs and road signs. These signs give directions. They tell how fast to go. They tell when to stop. They guide you to your destination.

Punctuation marks are like street and road signs. They tell readers when to start and when to stop. They tell readers when to slow down, that is, when to pause. Punctuation marks help guide readers to the writer's meaning.

Punctuation marks tell how to read lines. See for yourself. Pretend you are an actor. Look at the sentences below, and read each sentence aloud.

I did it?   I did it.   I did it!

What did the punctuation mark tell you about each sentence? The first sentence asked a question, the second sentence made a simple statement, and the third sentence exclaimed what the writer did. The meaning of each sentence is very different from the others, but you would never have known what the writer was trying to say without the correct punctuation mark.

Everyone has trouble with punctuation from time to time. It's not always easy to know when and where to place a comma or how to use quotation marks correctly. This book offers

quick, simple explanations of the punctuation marks you are learning in school. It also teaches you how and when to capitalize words. If you get confused by punctuation and capitalization while doing your schoolwork, this book will come to the rescue.

What's the best way to use this book? A quick look at the Contents will tell you which chapter covers the area you're working on or interested in. Flip through the chapter until you come across the material you need. Answers for all the quizzes are at the end of each chapter. Another way to find what you're looking for is to search for key words in the Index on page 144. The Index will tell you where to go by giving you the page numbers of important subjects, such as "abbreviations" and "contractions."

This book will serve as a useful reference for you as you move up through the grades. Keep it handy. Use it when you write or when you go through your written work. The more you use it, the better you'll do in school.

This book is also written to keep you laughing as well as learning. It's filled with interesting facts, challenging riddles, hilarious jokes, and amusing illustrations. Some people think it's so much fun that they read it again and again!

Periods, Question Marks, and Exclamation Points
The End?!

The three end punctuation marks may be different, but they have one thing in common. They tell the reader to come to a full stop before going on to the next sentence.

> ## The sentence ends here.?!

End of a Sentence

The following sentences have the same words, but they have different meanings. They show just how important end punctuation marks are.

She was parking the car in the house. He was reading.

She was parking the car. In the house, he was reading.

The rule for end punctuation is very simple: You must always use a punctuation mark at the end of a sentence. In this chapter, you'll learn when to use a period, a question mark, and an exclamation point.

Make Your Mark

Punctuation marks make words and sentences easier to read and understand. End marks give important information. A **period** shows you are making a statement or giving a polite command.

I ate the pie.

My sister likes ice cream.

Please bring the eggs.

A **question mark** shows you are asking a question.

Did I eat the pie?

Where is the ice cream?

Did you drop the eggs?

An **exclamation point** shows that you feel strongly about what you are saying.

Yes! I ate the pie!

The ice cream melted!

The eggs broke!

Slipups

Where Is the Question?
Some people think sentences with the words *who, what, where, when, why,* and *how* always take question marks.

What a great smile you have? How tall you are?

This is wrong. These words can signal questions, but they can also be used in other ways. Here *what* and *how* are used in an exclamation. These sentences need an exclamation point.

What a great smile you have! How tall you are!

Try It

Complete these sentences by adding end punctuation marks.

1. Get out of my way

2. What time does the show start

3. How many people did you invite

4. What beautiful butterflies

5. The puppy licked her face

6. How rude

7. I don't believe it

8. Sherlock Holmes is a well-known detective

9. Please whisper in the library

10. Where did you leave your backpack

Answers are on page 19.

RIDDLE?

When is a question not a question?

Actually it is always a question, but when it is an indirect question, the sentence ends with a period, not a question mark. For example, "She asked me to come to her house." It's not really asking a question, so beware of questions that don't ask direct questions.

Wow! Interjections!

You know that a sentence with an exclamation point expresses a strong feeling. Certain words or groups of words can express a strong feeling, too. They are called **interjections**. Interjections express emotions, such as surprise, anger, pain, and relief.

Common Interjections		
ah	okay	well
aha	ouch	whoops
hey	ow	wow
shh	oh	ugh
oh no	uh-oh	hooray

Use an **exclamation point** after an interjection that expresses a strong feeling. Use a **comma** after an interjection that expresses a mild feeling.

Wow! That was a great game!

Hooray! I got the part!

Okay, let's continue the game.

Whoops, I dropped the pie.

Slipups

One Is Enough

You're excited, and you want to show it. You add a few exclamation points to the end of your sentence.

We won the game in the final second!!!

Wrong! It's not correct to use more than one end punctuation mark. A single exclamation point signals excitement. You don't need more than one exclamation point.

We won the game in the final second!

Try It

How should each sentence be punctuated? Add exclamation points, commas, and capital letters where you think they are needed.

1. Hey that's mine!

2. Shh I can't hear the speaker.

3. Ouch I burned my hand.

4. Oh no I dropped my popcorn.

5. Uh-oh let's get out of here.

Answers are on page 19.

Take the Challenge

PRIVATE NO SWIMMING ALLOWED

Can you use three punctuation marks to turn this statement into a public invitation?

Answer is on page 19.

Fragments and Run-ons

You may know what the different end punctuation marks are, but many people have trouble knowing when a sentence is a sentence.

A sentence is a complete thought.

A sentence has a subject. The **subject** of a sentence names someone or something.

> **The puppy** licks my face.

A sentence has a predicate (phrase with a verb). The **predicate** tells what the subject is or does.

> The puppy **licks my face.**

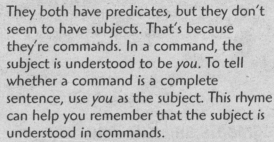

Tricks

You Are Understood

Are these sentences fragments?

Stop!
Don't go in there!

They both have predicates, but they don't seem to have subjects. That's because they're commands. In a command, the subject is understood to be *you*. To tell whether a command is a complete sentence, use *you* as the subject. This rhyme can help you remember that the subject is understood in commands.

It's you that always takes command,
or so I've been led to understand.

Sentence Fragments

A *sentence fragment* is not a sentence because it does not express a complete thought.

at school   my brother Phil   went dancing

For a sentence to be complete, it needs a subject and a predicate.

Who is at school? **What happened** at school?

What about my brother Phil? **What did he do?**

Who went dancing?

Fragments are usually missing one part or the other, and sometimes they are missing both. Sentence fragments are easy

to correct. Just ask yourself *who?* and *what happened?*
Make sure the sentence answers both questions.

Fragment	Correct Sentence
But came in last.	**Al ran well,** but came in last.
Went to the track.	**We went to the track.**
After the race.	After the race, **the winner got a medal.**

Try It

Add words to the fragments to make complete sentences.

1. one funny story

2. were sleeping in the beachhouse

3. a book of tall tales

4. breaststroke, backstroke, and butterfly

5. this big, furry animal

6. went all the way to the museum

7. drank juice every morning

8. have many books to read

Answers will vary.

Run-On Sentences

A **run-on sentence** happens when two or more sentences run together. Run-on sentences may have commas or no punctuation at all.

> Sheila looked around, she didn't see her friends anywhere.

You can correct a run-on sentence in one of three ways.

You can use end punctuation and a capital letter to divide a run-on sentence into two sentences.

> Sheila looked around. She didn't see her friends anywhere.

You can use a comma and a conjunction (the words *and*, *but*, and *or* are conjunctions) to join related sentences.

> Sheila looked around, **but** she didn't see her friends anywhere.

You can use a semicolon (;) to separate the run-on sentence into two sentences. (See how a semicolon is used on pages 73–74.)

> Sheila looked around; she didn't see her friends anywhere.

Usually you can divide a run-on sentence into two sentences, but using a conjunction or a semicolon depends on what you are trying to say.

Go For It!

You're on a roll. Correct these run-on sentences as many ways as you can.

1. June's bicycle needs repairs she can't fix it herself.

2. The parade was going by the floats were beautiful.

3. The smoke alarm went off the firefighters were there in a minute.

4. Now Rusty has two of the same CDs I want to borrow one.

5. Lizzie plays the flute she is in the band.

6. My five friends are here they like to go rollerblading.

7. Everyone will vote the election will be close.

8. Jim went into the pool everyone watched him dive.

9. We went to the museum we saw Egyptian mummies.

Answers will vary.

Don't Be Scared Off!

Do you carve pumpkins on Halloween? Did you ever wonder how this custom got started? You can find out by reading the following story. You'll have to take your time, though. The story has many sentence fragments and run-on sentences. Correct them while you read.

- -

Today, most people think. Halloween is a lot of fun but hundreds of years ago, it was a frightening night, it was said that ghosts roamed the earth. on Halloween night. To protect themselves from these ghosts. People lit bonfires they hoped the fires would drive the ghosts away.

Some people did. more than that they wanted to keep a fire right in front of their homes. So they made jack-o'-lanterns in those days. "jack" was a common name for "man." Jack-o'-lantern meant *man with a lantern*, or night watchman.

In Scotland. children carved jack-o'-lanterns

from large turnips. And put lighted candles inside them. When Europeans came to America. they brought the custom with them but they carved pumpkins instead of turnips.

Times have changed. Over the years. Today, the only Halloween "ghosts" are trick-or-treaters folks light jack-o'-lanterns to welcome these ghosts. Not to scare them away.

Answers are on page 19.

TIP FOR THE DAY!
Remember! If you use too many exclamation points, they lose their punch!

What's happening in this picture? What do you think each kid is feeling? Write the punctuation mark you would use in the speech balloon for each kid.

Summing It Up

- A **sentence** has a subject and a predicate and expresses a complete thought.

- A **sentence fragment** does not express a complete thought. It is usually missing the subject, the predicate, or both.

- A **run-on sentence** is two or more sentences that run together in one sentence.

Answers

Page 8

TRY IT

1) Get out of my way!; 2) What time does the show start?; 3) How many people did you invite?; 4) What beautiful butterflies!; 5) The puppy licked her face.; 6) How rude!; 7) I don't believe it!; 8) Sherlock Holmes is a well-known detective.; 9) Please whisper in the library.; 10) Where did you leave your backpack?

Page 10

TRY IT

1) Hey! That's mine!; 2) Shh, I can't hear the speaker. (or !); 3) Ouch! I burned my hand.; 4) Oh no, I dropped my popcorn.; 5) Uh-oh, let's get out of here. (or !)

Page 11

TAKE THE CHALLENGE
PRIVATE? NO! SWIMMING ALLOWED.

Pages 16–17

DON'T BE SCARED OFF!

Today, most people think Halloween is a lot of fun, but hundreds of years ago, it was a frightening night. It was said that ghosts roamed the earth on Halloween night. To protect themselves from these ghosts, people lit bonfires. They hoped the fires would drive the ghosts away.

Some people did more than that. They wanted to keep a fire right in front of their homes, so they made jack-o'-lanterns. In those days, "jack" was a common name for "man." Jack-o'-lantern meant *man with a lantern,* or night watchman.

In Scotland, children carved jack-o'-lanterns from large turnips and put lighted candles inside them. When Europeans came to America, they brought the custom with them, but they carved pumpkins instead of turnips.

Times have changed over the years. Today, the only Halloween "ghosts" are trick-or-treaters. Folks light jack-o'-lanterns to welcome these ghosts, not to scare them away.

Other Uses for Periods
It's Not Just for the Ending

The period is used to signal the end of a sentence. But there are other uses for periods. Find out what they are.

When to Use a Period

In Chapter One, you learned that periods can be used at the end of a sentence. Periods are also used with initials, as decimal points, and with many abbreviations.

WITH INITIALS:

Booker T. Washington

E. B. White

J. Lopez

AS A DECIMAL POINT:

The class collected $55.30 at the book drive.

When my temperature hit 102.1 degrees, I felt very sick.

WITH SOME ABBREVIATIONS:

Mr.   etc.   A.M.   Jr.   Rd.

Tip

When an abbreviation appears at the end of a sentence, use only one period.

I play soccer at the park on Palmer Ave.

Take Note!

Some abbreviations do not have periods. Refer to your dictionary to learn more.

VCR　videocassette recorder
FBI　Federal Bureau of Investigation
mph　miles per hour
m　meter
ATM　automatic teller machine

Slipups

Happy Endings

Will you fly with me to Washington, D.C.

At first glance, you might think this sentence is correct, but take a closer look. It is a question. It needs a question mark.

Will you fly with me to Washington, D.C.?

Remember, even when a question ends with an abbreviation that takes a period, you still need to add the question mark.

(By the way, D.C. is the abbreviation for District of Columbia.)

Try It

Correct these sentences by adding periods.

1. I am reading a book by C S Lewis.

2. The movie starts at 5:00 P M

3. The skating rink is at 220 S Cedar St

4. Michael J Fox is a popular actor.

5. Jim A Bailey, Jr , is the son of Jim A Bailey, Sr.

6. Books by A A Milne are Mrs Lee's favorites.

7. I have only $2 00 in my pocket.

8. Normal human body temperature is 98 6 degrees.

9. I like apples, oranges, bananas, etc

Answers are on page 29.

Where Should a Period Go?

IT'S VERY IMPORTANT TO KNOW WHERE TO PLACE A PERIOD BECAUSE YOU WANT TO MAKE SURE THAT WHAT YOU SAY IS WHAT YOU MEAN.

A period placed in the wrong place can really change what is being said.

WHERE YOU PLACE A PERIOD IN A NUMBER CAN ALSO MAKE A BIG DIFFERENCE.
In fact, it can be the difference between running one mile and one hundred miles.

How many miles did you run today?

1.003 miles   10.03 miles   100.3 miles

Speaking of Numbers

An odd abbreviation with a period is No., which is sometimes used as an abbreviation for *number*. What is odd about this abbreviation is that there is no "o" in number.

Laugh Break

Read the following funny story, and place periods where they belong.

Mr I M Rich had lots of money He liked to collect antiques One day, he went into an antique shop and saw a beautiful grandfather clock "How much do you want for that clock?" he asked the owner

"It costs $2,999 99," the owner said.

"I'll take it," Mr Rich said, giving the owner a check The clock was large, but Mr Rich lifted it onto his shoulder and walked away

A woman and her dog were standing at the corner She had her back to Mr Rich When Mr Rich reached the corner, he stopped to look for traffic He turned one way and then the other The clock swung around and hit the woman in the head The woman fell down

Mr I M Rich put down the clock and helped the woman get up "I'm sorry," he said "I didn't see you"

"That's all right," the woman said Then she noticed the grandfather clock and asked, "Why can't you wear a watch like other people?"

Answers are on page 29.

Outlines

When you write an outline for a school report, remember to use **capital letters** and **periods** correctly.

CAPITALIZE THE FIRST WORD IN EVERY LINE OF AN OUTLINE.

USE A PERIOD AFTER EACH NUMBER OR LETTER SEPARATING ITEMS IN AN OUTLINE.

Wolfgang Amadeus Mozart (1756–1791)

I.   Childhood

    A. Born in Salzburg, Austria

    B. Taught music by his father

    C. Showed talent early

       1. Played harpsichord at age 4

       2. Wrote music at age 5

       3. Performed with his older sister on tours throughout Europe

II. Adulthood

    A. Lived in Vienna, Austria

    B. Composed music and performed

       1. Not able to support family

       2. Died poor at age 36

III. Achievements

    A. Wrote more than 600 compositions and 22 operas

    B. Music withstood test of time

        1. His music is played around the world today

        2. Summer music festivals honor him

If you need to add more information under a number, such as "1" or "2," use lowercase letters ("a," "b," "c," and so on), and then use lowercase Roman numerals ("i," "ii," "iii," and so on) under the lowercase letters.

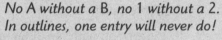

Tricks

It Takes Two
No A without a B, no 1 without a 2.
In outlines, one entry will never do!

This little rhyme can help you write outlines. If you are going to list subheadings in your outline, be sure you have at least two. Never use a subheading if you have only one supporting detail for an entry. This means that you may have a Roman numeral without an A and B or an A without a *1, 2, 3*, and you must have at least two Roman numerals (I, II) in an outline.

Create an Outline

Use the following words to create an outline on a separate sheet of paper:

strings, Carol, drum, Jim, boys, bass, Kenny, instruments, Suzie, musicians, violin, flute, Ron, others, trumpet, girls, Kathy, harp

Answers are on page 29.

Pop Quiz!

Answer the questions by placing the correct answers in the blanks and then writing the letter of that answer next to the question. Be sure to put periods where they are needed.

Questions:

1. How much money is a five-dollar bill and two dimes? ___

2. What is the abbreviation of road in Cherry Road? ___

3. What time is it at noon? ___

4. Who became President of the United States after Bill Clinton? ___

5. What is the abbreviation of mister? ___

6. If it is five miles to the store and you run half the distance, how far have you run? (Answer with a decimal point.) ___

Answers:

a. _____   d. _____ miles

b. _____ ___ _____   e. Cherry ___

c. $_____   f. ___ o'clock ___M.

Answers are on page 29.

Answers

<u>Page 22</u>

Try It
1) C. S.; 2) P.M.; 3) S., St.; 4) J.;
5) A., Jr., A.; 6) A. A., Mrs.;
7) $2.00; 8) 98.6; 9) etc.

<u>Page 24</u>

Laugh Break
Mr. I. M. Rich had lots of money. He liked to collect antiques. One day, he went into an antique shop and saw a beautiful grandfather clock. "How much do you want for that clock?" he asked the owner.

"It costs $2,999.99," the owner said.

"I'll take it," Mr. Rich said, giving the owner a check. The clock was large, but Mr. Rich lifted it onto his shoulder and walked away.

A woman and her dog were standing at the corner. She had her back to Mr. Rich. When Mr. Rich reached the corner, he stopped to look for traffic. He turned one way and then the other. The clock swung around and hit the woman in the head. The woman fell down.

Mr. I. M. Rich put down the clock and helped the woman get up. "I'm sorry," he said. "I didn't see you."

"That's all right," the woman said. Then she noticed the grandfather clock and asked, "Why can't you wear a watch like other people?"

<u>Page 27</u>

Create an Outline
I. Musicians
  A. Girls
      1. Carol
      2. Kathy
      3. Suzie
  B. Boys
      1. Jim
      2. Kenny
      3. Ron
II. Instruments
  A. Strings
      1. Bass
      2. Harp
      3. Violin
  B. Others
      1. Drum
      2. Flute
      3. Trumpet

<u>Page 28</u>

Pop Quiz!
1) c, $5.20; 2) e, Cherry Rd.; 3) f, 12 o'clock P.M.; 4) b, George W. Bush; 5) a, Mr.; 6) d, 2.5 miles

Commas
It's Time to Pause

One comma can be very important in a sentence. Like the period, the comma is a signal. The period says, "Stop here." The comma, on the other hand, says, "Pause here."

Commas in a Series

The following two sentences have the same words, but they have different meanings.

Mary Jane and Amy each rowed.

Mary, Jane, and Amy each rowed.

Here's another pair of sentences. One sentence mentions three items of food; the other sentence mentions four. Which sentence matches the picture below?

They ate ice cream, chocolate, cake, and cookies.

They ate ice cream, chocolate cake, and cookies.

Challenge

Can you think of more than one way to punctuate the following sentence?

For lunch they had fruit salad spaghetti and meatballs bread and butter cookies and ice cream.

Answers are on page 50.

Use a comma to separate three or more words, phrases, or ideas in a series.

I enjoy soccer, baseball, and tennis.

The cat dashed across the street, over the grass, and inside our house.

The answers are 3, 11, 47, and 64.

Favorites

Answer these questions in complete sentences.

1. What are your favorite foods?

2. What are your favorite colors?

3. What are your favorite school subjects?

Answers will vary.

A compound sentence is a sentence made up of two or more independent clauses. An independent clause is a clause that can stand alone as a sentence, such as, "I slept on the couch." A dependent clause is a clause that cannot stand alone as a sentence, such as, "because I was tired." The dependent clause relies on the independent clause to make sense. By putting the two clauses together, it makes sense: "I slept on the couch because I was tired."

Use a comma to separate two or more independent clauses that are connected by a conjunction.

> Johnny is in the classroom, Heather is playing softball, and Chris is at the computer.

> Flowers are blooming, snow has covered the ground, or rain has flooded the area.

Serial Comma

Some people use a comma to separate the last two items in a series: "Cars, trains, and planes." This comma is known as the "serial comma." Other people don't use a comma to separate the last two items in a series: "Cars, trains and planes." Either is correct. But don't do both in the same assignment. Otherwise, it can be confusing to the reader.

Try It

Correct these sentences by placing commas where they belong.

1. Let's go to the zoo see where the animals roam and talk for hours.

2. I took pictures in the morning at dusk and in the evening.

3. The tree was old thick and sturdy.

4. Joe baked the cookies Sasha made the cake and I made the pudding.

5. We had bacon and eggs cereal and toast for breakfast.

6. The hamster ran under the chair across the floor and around the table.

Answers are on page 50.

Cool, "Comma," and Collected

Use a comma between two or more adjectives that come before a noun.

It was a run-down, crooked house.

She drove a shiny, two-door car.

Murphy is a really happy, friendly dog.

Use a comma before *and, but,* or *or* when the word is used to join two independent clauses.

Murphy was a huge dog, **and** Jess could hardly hold on to him.

Tip

Sometimes you don't use a comma between two adjectives. Here's how you decide: If you place *and* between the adjectives or if you reverse the adjectives and it still sounds right, you use a comma. Otherwise, you don't.

Awkward: I bought an expensive and Japanese camera.

Awkward: I bought a Japanese expensive camera.

Correct: I bought an expensive Japanese camera.

Jess tried to pull Murphy away, **but** Murphy kept right on going.

Either Murphy got away from Jess and knocked over the boxes, **or** Jess lost his balance and fell into the boxes.

Slipups

No Comma Relief Needed
Sara rode her bike to school, and put it into the bicycle rack.

Oops! No comma is needed here. The words *and, but,* and *or* never take a comma when they join two predicates with the same subject.

Remember, be careful not to separate predicates from their subject.
Sara rode her bike to school and put it into the bicycle rack.

Use a comma when you write large numbers.

The blue whale is huge. It weighs more than 1,500 pounds!

The lottery ticket was worth 1,000,000 dollars.

Tricks

Commas in Numbers

4922368501

Can you read the number above? Are there millions or billions? Without commas, the number is hard to read. You can fix this by adding commas. But how do you know where to put the commas? That's easy. Start at the right, and count 3 digits. Then add a comma.

4922368,501

Count and add commas until you can no longer count three digits.

4,922,368,501

It's easier to read the number now, isn't it?

Try It

Correct these sentences by adding commas where they are needed.

1. There are 1628 jelly beans in the jar.

2. My dad loves his soft comfortable reclining chair.

3. There was room for everyone in the elevator but Sam offered to wait for the next one anyway.

4. Was Marsha really angry at Leon or was she just pretending to be angry?

5. Mark's car was still going strong after 150000 miles.

6. It was a dark dingy room.

7. Wait your turn and then you can eat.

Answers are on page 50.

Commas in Quotes

Use a comma to separate a short exclamation from the rest of the sentence.

"Hey, what's for dinner?"

"Oh, I'm just fine."

Change the meaning of the following quote by adding a comma.

"No one can be happy without money and fame."

Answer is on page 50.

Use a comma to set off someone's exact words.

As my mother always says, "No news is good news."

"The test is on Friday," said the teacher.

Use a comma to set off the name of a person someone is talking to.

"Ms. Bell, how are you?"

"Please, Charlie, shut the door."

Try It

Correct these sentences by adding commas where they are needed.

1. "Ben when will you be ready to leave?"

2. Judy always says "Better late than never."

3. "Wow I never skip a meal."

4. "If you like" he said "you can come."

5. "Get in the car Becky."

Answers are on page 50.

Write the Wrongs!

1. At three o'clock, let's leave Mindy.

Change the punctuation so that Mindy comes, too.

2. Mary Beth, Jill, and Julie are friends of Kelly.

Add a comma so that Kelly has four friends.

3. Toby took 19348 sports cards to the convention.

Add a comma to make it more clear how many cards Toby took.

4. I walked down the long winding road.

Change the punctuation so you know the road is long.

5. Susan also brought fresh bananas, candy apples, and sliced oranges.

Susan was supposed to have brought four items. Make sure that she does.

Answers are on page 50.

Mark My Words!

Below are pairs of questions and answers. Choose the letter of the answer that matches each question.

___1. Are you writing, Pete?

___2. Are you writing Pete?

a. Yes, I'm writing my school report.

b. No, I'll phone him instead.

___3. Can Betty Lou and Tom watch the movie with us?

___4. Can Betty, Lou, and Tom watch the movie with us?

a. Well, it would be pretty crowded with three more.

b. Sure, there are two seats left.

___5. Hide the diamond ring now, and wait.

___6. Hide the diamond, ring now, and wait.

a. Cover your finger.

b. Listen for the door buzzer.

Answers are on page 51.

Get the Point?

The sentence pairs below are the same except for their punctuation. Which sentence answers each question?

1. Which sentence is a command?

a. ____ Jenn and Joe, come with me.

b. ____ Jenn and Joe come with me.

2. Which sentence is said to Bob?

a. ____ We are going to cook Bob before we die of hunger.

b. ____ We are going to cook, Bob, before we die of hunger.

3. Which sentence likes the way Dahlia looks?

a. ____ Dahlia is a pretty, smart girl.

b. ____ Dahlia is a pretty smart girl.

Answers are on page 51.

More Uses for Commas

Use commas to set off introductory phrases or clauses at the beginning of the sentence.

On the kitchen table, I placed the carton of milk.

Beside the batting cage, they threw their mitts.

After Lisa finished her homework, she watched TV.

As I slept, I dreamed I was a prince.

Use commas to separate "interrupters" from the rest of the sentence.

You know, of course, what to do.

Jean, by the way, are you coming tonight?

A dog, for example, can be a good friend.

Sign of the Times

Watch out for a funny sign! Where would you add a comma?

DUE TO STRIKE
GRAVE DIGGING
DONE BY
SKELETON CREW

Answer is on page 51.

Fun with Commas

While we eat the rabbits sit quietly.

Yikes! These rabbits need your help. Save them by adding a comma to the right place in the sentence.

Answer is on page 51.

Use commas to set off words that add information about the noun that comes directly before them.

Jamal, the class secretary, will now take attendance.

The principal, Mrs. Walker, spoke to the teachers.

Wendy, my best friend, rode on a train.

WE INTERRUPT

Here are a few common interrupters. Use commas before and after them in a sentence.

by the way	for example
indeed	I think
after all	therefore
however	in fact
of course	I believe

Try It

Add commas where they belong in these sentences.

1. After spring break I went back to school.

2. When you call a representative will speak to you.

3. It's chilly after all so wear your jacket.

4. You know by the way that I won't be here tomorrow.

5. If the phone rings please answer it.

6. Mr. Oaks the plumber fixed our pipes in the bathroom.

7. The boat however will not sink.

8. Bring your car the red convertible to my house.

9. In the bedroom by the pool my brother hid my tape.

10. I could have brought my cousin Teddy.

Answers are on page 51.

Commas Add Up to FUN

Now that you know the rules for using commas, have some fun with the following sentences.

1. **a.** Here's some, honey.
   b. Here's some honey.
   Which sentence expresses affection?

2. **a.** Pat, the snob, is here.
   b. Pat, the snob is here.
   Which sentence would make Pat angry?

3. **a.** Are you lifting Ted for exercise?
   b. Are you lifting, Ted, for exercise?
   Which sentence asks if Ted is using weights?

4. **a.** Swallowing Dr. Welby hurts my throat.
   b. Swallowing, Dr. Welby, hurts my throat.
   Which sentence puts the doctor in danger?

5. **a.** What's wrong when a motor keeps missing Al?
   b. What's wrong when a motor keeps missing, Al?
   Which sentence suggests that Al is a mechanic?

6. **a.** Is it my turn to cook, Dad?
   b. Is it my turn to cook Dad?
   Which sentence is really gross?

7. **a.** Painting in my view is not a good idea.
   b. Painting, in my view, is not a good idea.
   Which sentence makes it difficult for the speaker to see?

Answers are on page 51.

It's a Date!

Use a comma to separate the date and the year. Use commas to separate the year from the date and the rest of the following sentence.

> The Declaration of Independence was signed on July 4, 1776.

> The tree was planted on May 12, 1998, in our backyard.

BUT

Do not use commas if you are giving only the month and the year.

> The weather in July 1776 was unusually warm.

Use a comma between the name of a city or town and the name of a state or country. If place names are within the sentence, also use a comma after the name of the state or country.

> The Liberty Bell is in Philadelphia, Pennsylvania.

> Philadelphia, Pennsylvania, is on the East Coast.

> Rome, Italy, has many beautiful buildings.

Try It

Add commas where they are needed in the following sentences.

1. Mother Hubbard opened the cupboard but it was bare.

2. Oh her poor dog won't get a bone.

3. How does your garden grow Mary?

4. All the flowers grow in a row of course.

5. In the early morning Jack and Jill went up the hill.

6. They wanted to fetch some cool clean water.

7. He was also wearing his shirt pants and one shoe.

8. I asked "Pussy Cat where have you been?"

9. He said that he went to London England to see the queen.

Answers are on page 51.

Addresses

When an address appears within a sentence, use a comma after each item in the address except the state.

My new address is 1717 Lakeview Drive, Denver, Colorado 80207.

BUT

Do not use a comma between items in an address that are joined by a preposition, such as *at* and *in*.

We visited the Empire State Building **at** 350 5th Avenue **in** New York, New York.

We will see Mt. Rushmore **in** South Dakota.

Use a comma after the greeting and the closing in friendly letters.

Dear Linda,

Your friend,

Who Am I?

Do you know how to use commas when you write dates and places? See for yourself by answering these questions.

Where were you born?_____

Where do you live?_____

When were you born?_____

When is the next time your school will be closed to celebrate a holiday?_____

Answers will vary.

Commas in a Letter

There are eight commas missing in the following letter. Can you find all the places where commas are needed?

100 Maple Avenue
Tulsa OK 74074

July 22, 2004

May Turner
220 Market Street
Lexington KY 40599

Dear Aunt May

Thank you very much for my birthday present. Now I have a cool case for all my CDs.

You have a good memory. Yes, I was born on May 14 1994 in Cleveland Ohio. You remembered that my parents lived there for a while when they were first married.

We're looking forward to your visit. You'll also be able to see Bobbie Jean. She lives at 660 Clinton Drive in Norman Oklahoma. We'll drive you to her house. That's a good way to see the sights, too!

See you soon.

Your niece

Olivia

Answers are on page 52.

Here's a bonus question for you. Add commas where they are needed and circle your answer.

Do the sentences in the last "Try It" on page 46 refer to folktales nursery rhymes or fairy tales?

Answers are on page 52.

Summing It Up

- Use commas to separate items in a series.

- Use commas between two or more adjectives that come before a noun.

- Use commas after words, phrases, and clauses that come at the beginning of a sentence.

- Use commas to separate the people spoken to from the rest of the sentence.

- Use commas to set off interrupters from the rest of the sentence.

- Use commas to set off additional, but not necessary, information about a noun.

Answers

Page 31

Challenge

Two possibilities are: For lunch they had fruit, salad, spaghetti and meatballs, bread and butter, cookies, and ice cream; For lunch they had fruit salad, spaghetti and meatballs, bread, and butter cookies, and ice cream.

Page 33

Try It

1) Let's go to the zoo, see where the animals roam, and talk for hours.; 2) I took pictures in the morning, at dusk, and in the evening.; 3) The tree was old, thick, and sturdy.; 4) Joe baked the cookies, Sasha made the cake, and I made the pudding.; 5) We had bacon and eggs, cereal, and toast for breakfast.; 6) The hamster ran under the chair, across the floor, and around the table.

Page 36

Try It

1) There are 1,628 jelly beans in the jar.; 2) My dad loves his soft, comfortable reclining chair.; 3) There was room for everyone .in the elevator, but Sam offered to wait for the next one anyway.; 4) Was Marsha really angry at Leon, or was she just pretending to be angry?; 5) Mark's car was still going strong after 150,000 miles.; 6) It was a dark, dingy room.; 7) Wait your turn, and then you can eat.

Change the Meaning

"No, one can be happy without money and fame."

Page 37

Try It

1) "Ben, when will you be ready to leave?"; 2) Judy always says, "Better late than never.";
3) "Wow, I never skip a meal.";
4) "If you like," he said, "you can come."; 5) "Get in the car, Becky."

Page 38

Write the Wrongs!

1). At three o'clock, let's leave, Mindy.; 2) Mary, Beth, Jill, and Julie are friends of Kelly.; 3) Toby took 19,348 sports cards to the convention.; 4) I walked down the long, winding road.; 5) Susan also brought fresh bananas, candy, apples, and sliced oranges.

Page 39

Mark My Words!
1) a; 2) b; 3) b; 4) a; 5) a; 6) b

Page 40

Get the Point?
1) a; 2) b; 3) a

Page 41

Sign of the Times
DUE TO STRIKE, GRAVE
DIGGING DONE BY SKELETON
CREW

Fun with Commas
While we eat, the rabbits sit
quietly.

Page 43

Try It
1) After spring break, I went back
to school.; 2) When you call, a
representative will speak to you.;
3) It's chilly, after all, so wear
your jacket.; 4) You know, by the
way, that I won't be here
tomorrow.; 5) If the phone rings,
please answer it.; 6) Mr. Oaks,
the plumber, fixed our pipes in
the bathroom.; 7) The boat,
however, will not sink.; 8) Bring
your car, the red convertible, to
my house.; 9) In the bedroom by
the pool, my brother hid my
tape.; 10) I could have brought
my cousin, Teddy.

Page 44

Commas Add Up to FUN
1) a; 2) a; 3) b; 4) a; 5) b; 6) b;
7) a

Page 46

Try It
1) Mother Hubbard opened the
cupboard, but it was bare.;
2) Oh, her poor dog won't get a
bone.; 3) How does your garden
grow, Mary?; 4) All the flowers
grow in a row, of course.; 5) In
the early morning, Jack and Jill
went up the hill.; 6) They wanted
to fetch some cool, clean water.;
7) He was also wearing his shirt,
pants, and one shoe.; 8) I asked,
"Pussy Cat, where have you
been?"; 9) He said that he went
to London, England, to see the
queen.

Page 48

Commas in a Letter
100 Maple Avenue
Tulsa, OK 74074

July 22, 2004

May Turner
220 Market Street
Lexington, KY 40599

Dear Aunt May,

Thank you very much for my birthday present. Now I have a cool case for all my CDs.

You have a good memory. Yes, I was born on May 14, 1994, in Cleveland, Ohio. You remembered that my parents lived there for a while when they were first married.

We're looking forward to your visit. You'll also be able to see Bobbie Jean. She lives at 660 Clinton Drive in Norman, Oklahoma. We'll drive you to her house. That's a good way to see the sights, too!

See you soon.

Your niece,
Olivia

Page 49

Bonus Question
Do the sentences in the last "Try It" on page 46 refer to folktales, nursery rhymes, or fairy tales?

Answer: nursery rhymes.

Quotation Marks
You Can Quote Me on It!

In this chapter, you'll learn about quotation marks and how commas and end punctuations are used inside and outside of quotation marks.

What Are They Really Saying?

"I cooked the spaghetti," said Denise in the pot!

Oh, no! Poor Denise. Can you think of a way to get her out of hot water? Try this:

"I cooked the spaghetti," said Denise, "in the pot!"

You can see that quotation marks can make a big difference.

What messy picture comes to mind when you read the following sentence?

"I like vanilla ice cream," said Sue, covered with fudge.

Can you think of a way to help get Sue cleaned up?

"I like vanilla ice cream," said Sue, "covered with fudge."

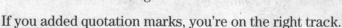

If you added quotation marks, you're on the right track.

When to Use Quotation Marks

Use quotation marks to show the exact words of a speaker, and use a comma or commas to set off the rest of the sentence from the speaker's words.

Chloe said, "I like peanut butter."

"I like peanut butter," said Chloe, "topped with banana."

"Peanut butter on top of a banana is really good," said Chloe.

Do not use a comma or quotation marks when you are just referring to what someone said.

Beth said she enjoyed the movie.

Try It

Add quotation marks and commas only if they are needed in the sentences below.

1. Someone once said No man is an island.

2. Ben Franklin said Early to bed, early to rise makes a man healthy, wealthy, and wise.

3. Sue told me she was hungry.

4. My favorite subjects are English and history said Chelsea in front of the school.

5. I like to go bowling said Stu whenever I can.

Answers are on page 66.

You Can Quote Me On It!

This exercise is fun. You'll see. Just copy the sentences on a separate sheet of paper, and follow the directions.

Jeff is always saying I'm lazy.

Punctuate this sentence to show that Jeff is talking about himself.

Ray said his boss is always late.

Punctuate this sentence to show that the boss is speaking.

The woman said the police officer was speeding.

Punctuate this sentence to show that the police officer is speaking.

Answers are on page 66.

In the Know

Place commas and periods *inside* the quotation marks.

"I'm hungry," she said.

She said, "I'm hungry."

Question marks and exclamation points go *inside* the quotation marks only if they belong to the quotation.

"Who took my pencil?" Alex asked.

"I hate liver!" Ray shouted.

Question marks and exclamation points are placed *outside* the quotation marks if they don't belong to the quotation.

Did she say "turn left" or "turn right"?

I can't believe he said "It doesn't matter"!

Try It

Punctuate these sentences.

1. Where are you going Bonnie asked.

2. Leave me alone Flynn shouted.

3. Do you agree that Haste makes waste

4. Dan said I'm almost finished with my homework

5. The teacher asked Are you ready for the test

Answers are on page 66.

Riddle Riot

What did the calculator say to the student?

"You can count on me."

Provide the correct answers and punctuation to the riddles below. The first one is done for you.

---

1. RIDDLE: What did the rug say to the floor?
The rug said, "I've got you covered."

2. RIDDLE: What did one candle say to the other?
_____ Are you going out tonight

3. RIDDLE: What did the apple tree tell the farmer?
_____ Stop picking on me

4. RIDDLE: What did one cornstalk tell the other?
_____ I'm all ears

5. RIDDLE: What did one elevator say to the other?
_____ I think I'm coming down with something

6. RIDDLE: What did the caterpillar say it would do for the new year?
_____ I'll turn over a new leaf

Answers are on page 66.

Jokers Wild

The conversations on this page will make you laugh. Match a question from Column A to its reply in Column B. Then punctuate the answer.

Column A	Column B
1. What should you say when a judge shouts "order"?	Lap dogs
2. "Why is a ball game a good place to be on a hot day?"	Actors are always in casts
3. "Why are fish smart?"	They always travel in schools
4. "What kind of dogs are the best swimmers?"	A hamburger and fries please
5. "How can you tell acting is dangerous?"	There are fans all around

Answers are on page 66.

More About School Reports

Underline (or italicize) the titles of books, magazines, newspapers, plays, and TV shows.

I found the ad in <u>The Daily News.</u>

I got most of my information from <u>Kids Discover</u> magazine.

Quotation Marks and Titles

Put quotation marks around the title of a **song, poem,** or **short story.**

> We rehearsed "This Land Is Your Land" all afternoon.

> "The Eagle," a poem by Tennyson, is my favorite.

RIDDLE

What punctuation mark is used in writing dance music?

Answer: The polka dot.

Tip

In printed materials, titles appear in italics. Italics are slanted letters: *The Red Pony.*

Put quotation marks around the title of a **magazine** or **newspaper article.**

> I read "Trading Baseball Cards" with great interest.

Put quotation marks around the title of a **chapter.**

> For homework, read "The Old West" in your textbook.

When you write a report, use quotation marks around words you copy from a book or other printed material.

> The ad said that the used bike was "in good condition."

Slipups

It Takes Two

Sometimes writers forget to add ending quotation marks.

The frog sings, "It isn't easy being green. I know what he means.

Without ending quotation marks, you don't know what the frog sings.

You need to show the end of the quotation.

The frog sings, "It isn't easy being green." I know what he means.

Remember, a quotation always takes two quotation marks—one beginning the quote and one ending the quote.

Tricks

Quotation Marks or Italics

Read the paragraph.

You may enjoy reading *Where the Sidewalk Ends* by Shel Silverstein. I really liked "Where the Sidewalk Ends."

Did you see that the same title is italicized in one place and has quotation marks in another? The writer seems confused. But is she?

Some poets name a book after one of the poems in it. If you are writing about the entire book, you italicize or underline the title. If you are writing about just the poem, you put the poem title in quotation marks.

Practice Makes Perfect

Use quotation marks in the following sentences.

1. My favorite song is Over the Rainbow.

2. I liked reading the magazine story called The Last Inning.

3. We should study the chapter The Growing Nation.

4. Hamburgers Aren't for Everyone is the title of the newspaper article.

5. Lisa read her poem, Spring Is Here, to our class.

6. Not in Today is the famous line in the book.

7. I want everyone to read my short story, You Can If You Try.

Answers are on page 66–67.

Funny Business

"How's business?"

"It's picking up," said the garbage collector.

Can you spot the humor in this conversation? Are you ready for more? Some snappy answers are in the box below. Match the answers to the workers. Use correct punctuation. The first one is done for you.

It's just fine, fine, fine

I'm running out of patience   It's grand   It's pointless

It always lets me down   It's a zoo   It's no joke

1. **"It's just fine, fine, fine,"**   said the judge.

2. _____   said the pencil salesperson.

3. _____   said the doctor.

4. _____ said the comedian.

5. _____ said the game warden.

6. _____ said the elevator operator.

7. _____ said the piano salesperson.

Answers are on page 67.

Quotations and Paragraphs

Begin a new paragraph for the quotation of each new speaker.

"Why aren't you working?" Sue asked Stu.

"My boss and I had a fight," Stu said, "and she wouldn't take back what she said."

"What did she say?" Sue asked.

"You're fired."

Did you know...

The marks of punctuation were also known as points or stops.

Who's Talking?

Add quotation marks, end punctuation, and commas to the following joke.

It was very quiet in the library. The librarian heard something and when she looked up she saw that a dog had come in.

Hello, said the dog softly. "I wonder if you can help me. I would like some books by Mark Twain.

"You're . . . " the librarian said. She couldn't even finish her sentence

"Maybe you didn't hear me the dog said a little louder. I'm looking for some books by Mark Twain.

The librarian stared at the dog. Then she screamed I can't believe it

I know said the dog. Almost nobody reads Mark Twain these days.

Answers are on page 67.

Looking Back

Punctuation marks in English were first used in the 16th century for *speech*. For example, the "full stop" or period (.) would mark the end of a sentence when a person prepared a speech.

It wasn't until the 17th century that punctuation marks *in print* came into practice. Then it became important to leave spaces between words, to indent the first line of a new paragraph, and to use capital letters to begin sentences and signal proper nouns.

Summing It Up

- Use quotation marks to show the exact words of a speaker.

- Put quotation marks around the title of a song, poem, or short story.

- Put quotation marks around the title of a magazine or newspaper article.

- Put quotation marks around the title of a chapter.

- Put quotation marks around words taken from a book or other printed material.

- Begin a new paragraph for the quotation of each new speaker.

Answers

Page 54

Try It
1) Someone once said, "No man is an island."; 2) Ben Franklin said, "Early to bed, early to rise makes a man healthy, wealthy, and wise."; 3) Sue told me she was hungry.; 4) "My favorite subjects are English and history," said Chelsea, in front of the school.; 5) "I like to go bowling," said Stu, "whenever I can."

Page 55

You Can Quote Me On It!
1) Jeff is always saying, "I'm lazy."; 2) "Ray," said his boss, "is always late."; 3) "The woman," said the police officer, "was speeding."

Page 56

Try It
1) "Where are you going?" Bonnie asked.; 2) "Leave me alone!" Flynn shouted.; 3) Do you agree that "Haste makes waste"?; 4) Dan said, "I'm almost finished with my homework."; 5) The teacher asked, "Are you ready for the test?"

Page 57

Riddle Riot
1) The rug said, "I've got you covered."; 2) One candle said to the other, "Are you going out tonight?"; 3) The apple tree told the farmer, "Stop picking on me."; 4) One cornstalk told the other, "I'm all ears."; 5) One elevator said to the other, "I think I'm coming down with something."; 6) The caterpillar said, "I'll turn over a new leaf."

Page 58

Jokers Wild
1) "A hamburger and fries, please."; 2) "There are fans all around."; 3) "They always travel in schools."; 4) "Lap dogs.";
5) "Actors are always in casts."

Page 61

Practice Makes Perfect
1) My favorite song is "Over the Rainbow."; 2) I liked reading the magazine story called "The Last Inning."; 3) We should study the chapter "The Growing Nation."; 4) "Hamburgers Aren't for Everyone" is the title of the

newspaper article.; 5) Lisa read her poem, "Spring Is Here," to our class.; 6) "Not in Today" is the famous line in the book.; 7) I want everyone to read my short story, "You Can If You Try."

Pages 62–63

Funny Business
1) "It's just fine, fine, fine," said the judge.; 2) "It's pointless," said the pencil salesperson.; 3) "I'm running out of patience," said the doctor.; 4) "It's no joke," said the comedian.; 5) "It's a zoo," said the game warden.; 6) "It always lets me down," said the elevator operator.; 7) "It's grand," said the piano salesperson.

Page 64

Who's Talking?
It was very quiet in the library. The librarian heard something, and when she looked up, she saw that a dog had come in.

"Hello," said the dog softly. "I wonder if you can help me. I would like some books by Mark Twain."

"You're . . ." the librarian said. She couldn't even finish her sentence.

"Maybe you didn't hear me," the dog said a little louder. "I'm looking for some books by Mark Twain."

The librarian stared at the dog. Then she screamed, "I can't believe it!"

"I know," said the dog. "Almost nobody reads Mark Twain these days."

Colons and Semicolons
Breaking Up Is Hard to Do

Colons and semicolons give writers more ways to punctuate sentences. In this chapter, you will learn, among other things, how they can replace a comma to give a sentence or phrase a different tone or pace.

When to Use a Colon

Use a colon to separate the hours from the minutes when you write the time.

> 7:30 A.M.   9:15 P.M.

Use a colon to introduce a statement.

> I always take Mom's advice: Get a good night's sleep before a test.

> Each day the teacher wrote this warning on the board: Come to class prepared.

Use a colon after the greeting in a business letter.

> Dear Ms. Thomas: Dear Sir or Madam:

An ad made this blooper:

Electric Razor for Men with Three Heads

Order, Order!

The following business letter contains several errors in punctuation. How many can you find?

June 14 2004
104 Easy St
Chicago IL 60606

Write Now Company
12 Lana Lane
Baltimore, MD 21213

Dear Sir or Madam
I would like to order the following two books

Raising Irish Setters
101 Things to Do with Chewing Gum

I am enclosing a check for $4.00. Would you please send me your latest catalog as well? Thank you.

Sincerely yours

Will I. Gettum

Answers are on page 80.

Slipups

Comma or Colon

Some writers use a comma after the greeting in a business letter.

Dear Ms. Sumter,

This is wrong. The greeting in a business letter is always followed by a colon.

Dear Ms. Sumter:

Remember, if your letter is not to a relative, a friend, or a pen pal, use a colon after the greeting.

Use a colon to introduce a list of items.

> For class, bring the following: a pen, a pencil, and a notebook.

> These are examples of what not to do in class: spit, scream, and punch another student.

> Here's what I want you to do before you go to bed: finish your homework, clean your room, and brush your teeth.

Do not use a colon after a verb or preposition, such as "in," "at," and "around."

> Among the birds we saw were robins, swallows, and a parrot.

> We saw many trees in the park, the forest, and our backyard.

> I like to read at home, school, and the library.

Try It

Put colons where they belong in these sentences.

1. I need to go to the store and buy a number of things milk, bread, cheese, and juice.

2. School starts at 8 20 A.M. and ends at 3 00 P.M.

3. The letter began as follows "To Whom It May Concern:".

4. Bring over the hot dogs, hamburgers, and steak.

5. After you hit the ball, do the following drop the bat, run to first, and tag the bag.

6. Dear Dr. Brown

7. She drove the car around the people, dogs, and bus.

Answers are on page 80.

Use a colon (not quotation marks) to introduce dialogue in a play.

Andrea: Why did you do that?

Henry: I'm sorry. I just wasn't thinking.

Use a colon when referring to a quotation.

Judy made a funny statement in class: "You're my favorite teacher because you look like Mr. Potato Head."

Do not use a colon when you're quoting someone.

> Judy said, "You're my favorite teacher because you look like Mr. Potato Head."

> Henry cried out, "Ouch! That really hurt!"

Try It

Put colons or commas where they belong in the sentences below.

1. I'll always remember what Mom said to me "Never tell a lie."

2. Joe said "I'll be back tomorrow."

3. He read this to me "A good person is never without friends."

4. I can't believe the umpire yelled "The game is canceled!"

5. Connie My backpack is too heavy.
   Bobby I'll carry your ruler.
   Connie Thanks a lot.
   Bobby No sweat.

Answers are on page 80.

The Semicolon

A semicolon works like a comma but shows more of a break than a comma.

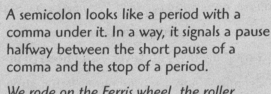

Tricks

Pause a Little Longer

A semicolon looks like a period with a comma under it. In a way, it signals a pause halfway between the short pause of a comma and the stop of a period.

We rode on the Ferris wheel, the roller coaster, and the merry-go-round; we ate a snack; and we saw a show. We had a great time at the fair!

Read aloud the sentences above. Pause a little longer after each semicolon than you do at the commas. But don't stop as long as you do at the end of the first sentence.

In a compound sentence, when two complete thoughts (independent clauses) are joined by the word *and, but, or, nor, for,* or *yet,* use a comma.

My dad is always late for work, nor is he early for dinner.

I didn't use the soap, for it's too rough on my skin.

Use a semicolon to join two or more independent clauses that may each stand alone as a separate sentence and are not joined by a conjunction.

The movie received great reviews; I can't wait to see it.

If the train comes, tell me; if it doesn't, don't tell me.

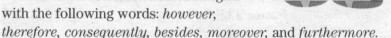

Use a semicolon to join two independent clauses when the second clause begins with the following words: *however, therefore, consequently, besides, moreover,* and *furthermore.*

I have a sore throat; therefore, I can't sing today.

I tried my best; however, I still need to practice.

Use a semicolon to separate phrases that already have commas in the phrase or phrases.

I brought my dog, Cody; my cat, Muffin; and my rabbit, Penny.

People should recycle papers, glass, and cans; shut off lights; and drive less to protect the environment.

Try It

Place semicolons where they belong in these sentences.

1. We invited Sue, the president Bert, the vice president Miriam, the treasurer and Pete, the secretary.

2. The team played well however, they didn't win.

3. It's raining therefore, the picnic is postponed.

4. Fred ordered chicken Alice ordered fish.

5. Our cat eats tuna our dog eats ground meat.

6. Diane pulled her horse to the water that stubborn horse just would not drink.

7. My brother loves to go to movies, basketball games, and concerts hates to work in the yard and the garage and complains whenever I'm around.

8. Mom went to shoe stores at the mall there weren't any shoes she liked.

Answers are on page 80.

Try It

Which sentence invited three people?

1. a. We invited John, the captain; Sue, the president; and Joe, the carpenter.
   b. We invited John, the captain, Sue, the president, Joe, and the carpenter.

Which sentence expects someone to speak up?

2. a. Ask not; to ask would be wrong.
   b. Ask; not to ask would be wrong.

Which sentence suggests that only apples are canned?

3. a. These fruits are canned: apples, sliced lemons, and peeled oranges.
   b. These fruits are canned apples, sliced lemons, and peeled oranges.

Answers are on page 80.

Two Little Pigs

Write the skit below on your own paper. Add colons and semicolons where they are needed. Don't use periods and commas.

1. Little Pig 1 Did you write your letter to the builder yet?

2. Little Pig 2 I just started writing. Here's what I have written so far

   Dear Mr. Wolfe

   I want to build a new home I need your help.

3. Little Pig 1 That's a good start however, your letter needs to name what materials you want to use.

4. Little Pig 2 I know. I want to use these materials bricks, mortar, fireproof shingles, and cement.

5. Little Pig 1 Be sure to remind him that there is a lot of huffing and puffing going on here therefore, your house needs to be windproof.

6. Little Pig 2 I will I'll also tell him about the town's noise law.

7. Little Pig 1 That's a good idea. What does that law say cannot be done before 7 00 A.M.?

8. Little Pig 2 Gardeners cannot use lawnmowers, leaf blowers, or electric clippers builders can't pound in nails and cement trucks can't mix cement before 7 00.

9. Little Pig 1 Well, I have to leave now. I'm going to visit Little Pig 3. He's building a house too however, he's using sticks.

10. Little Pig 2 I know. I think he is being foolish, but he once said to me "Why should I use expensive building materials when I can find sticks lying around everywhere?"

Answers are on page 81.

When you finish writing, get together with a friend. You can have fun performing the skit.

Clean This Mess!

Clean up this mess with a colon and semicolons.

I have a hard time doing these things. picking up leaves, grass, and rocks, eating vegetables, and sleeping on the floor, in a tent, and inside a dark room.

Answers are on page 81.

Summing It Up

- The colon is most often used to introduce a list or quotation.

- The colon is also used after the greeting in a business letter and between the hours and the minutes of a day.

- The semicolon joins two independent clauses when the second clause begins with the following words: however, therefore, consequently, besides, moreover, and furthermore.

- The semicolon is also used to separate phrases that have commas.

Stumpers!

Here's a test that covers everthing you've learned so far about punctuation. The exercises on this page are *super*-challenging. Stump your friends and family. Amaze your teachers! Punctuate these sentences so they make sense.

1. At 11 30 A.M. a pizza-eating contest attracted only two big eaters a teenage boy who ate 20 slices and a 92-year-old grandmother who won.

2. The outfielder caught the ball just as his head hit the wall the ball dropped to the ground and he picked it up and threw it to third

3. Can I have a round table asked the man with three legs

4. Machines will not tear your laundry we do it by hand

5. Before you put the baby on the carpet clean the floor with a vacuum cleaner

6. Help Bakers wanted from France

7. The spoons are made out of silver Peg

Answers are on page 81.

Answers

Page 69

Order, Order!
[six errors]
June 14, 2004
104 Easy St.
Chicago, IL 60606

Write Now Company
12 Lana Lane
Baltimore, MD 21213

Dear Sir or Madam:
I would like to order the following two books:
Raising Irish Setters
101 Things to Do with Chewing Gum
I am enclosing a check for $4.00. Would you please send me your latest catalog as well? Thank you.

Sincerely yours,

Will I. Gettum

Page 70–71

Try It
1) things:; 2) 8:20, 3:00;
3) follows:; 4) no colon;
5) following:; 6) Brown:; 7) no colon

Page 72

Try It
1) I'll always remember what Mom said to me: "Never tell a lie."; 2) Joe said, "I'll be back tomorrow."; 3) He read this to me: "A good person is never without friends."; 4) I can't believe the umpire yelled, "The game is canceled!"; 5) Connie: My backpack is too heavy. Bobby: I'll carry your ruler. Connie: Thanks a lot. Bobby: No sweat.

Pages 74–75

Try It
1) We invited Sue, the president; Bert, the vice president; Miriam, the treasurer; and Pete, the secretary.; 2) The team played well; however, they didn't win.; 3) It's raining; therefore, the picnic is postponed.; 4) Fred ordered chicken; Alice ordered fish.; 5) Our cat eats tuna; our dog eats ground meat.; 6) Diane pulled her horse to the water; that stubborn horse just would not drink.; 7) My brother loves to go to movies, basketball games, and concerts; hates to work in the yard and the garage; and complains whenever I'm around.; 8) Mom went to shoe stores at the mall; there weren't any shoes she liked.

Page 75

Try It
1) a; 2) b; 3) b

Pages 76–77

Two Little Pigs

1) Little Pig 1: Did you write your letter to the builder yet?

2) Little Pig 2: I just started writing. Here's what I have written so far:
Dear Mr. Wolfe:
I want to build a new home; I need your help.

3) Little Pig 1: That's a good start; however, your letter needs to name what materials you want to use.

4) Little Pig 2: I know. I want to use these materials: bricks, mortar, fireproof shingles, and cement.

5) Little Pig 1: Be sure to remind him that there is a lot of huffing and puffing going on here; therefore, your house needs to be windproof.

6) Little Pig 2: I will; I'll also tell him about the town's noise law.

7) Little Pig 1: That's a good idea. What does that law say cannot be done before 7:00 A.M.?

8) Little Pig 2: Gardeners cannot use lawnmowers, leaf blowers, or electric clippers; builders can't pound in nails; and cement trucks can't mix cement before 7:00.

9) Little Pig 1: Well, I have to leave now. I'm going to visit Little Pig 3. He's building a house too; however, he's using sticks.

10) Little Pig 2: I know. I think he is being foolish, but he once said to me: "Why should I use expensive building materials when I can find sticks lying around everywhere?"

Page 77

Clean This Mess!

I have a hard time doing these things: picking up leaves, grass, and rocks; eating vegetables; and sleeping on the floor, in a tent, and inside a dark room.

Pages 78–79

Stumpers!

1) At 11:30 A.M., a pizza-eating contest attracted only two big eaters: a teenage boy, who ate 20 slices, and a 92-year-old grandmother, who won.; 2) The outfielder caught the ball just as his head hit the wall; the ball dropped to the ground, and he picked it up and threw it to third.; 3) "Can I have a round table," asked the man, "with three legs?"; 4) Machines will not tear your laundry; we do it by hand.; 5) Before you put the baby on the carpet, clean the floor with a vacuum cleaner.; 6) Help! Bakers wanted from France!; 7) "The spoons are made out of silver, Peg."

Hyphens
Come Together

The hyphen joins two words. Hyphens are also used to divide words and to create new words.

Look at these two sentences:

At the zoo, we saw a man eating tiger.

At the zoo, we saw a man-eating tiger.

Which sentence says the tiger is the eater? (The second sentence.)

Slipups

One Is Enough
You're excited, and you want to show it. You add a few exclamation points to the end of your sentence.

We won the game in the final second!!!

Wrong! It's not correct to use more than one end punctuation mark. A single exclamation point signals excitement. You don't need more than one exclamation point.

We won the game in the final second!

Tip

A dictionary shows how to divide words into syllables. Dots or spaces show where hyphens would go.

men • tion
sick • ness

When to Use Hyphens

Use a hyphen to divide a word when you run out of room at the end of a line. But remember, a word can be divided only between its syllables. One-syllable words can't be divided. A syllable is any part of a word that has a vowel sound. For example, "sep•a•rate" has three syllables and three vowel sounds.

> After school, we all walk home to-
>
> gether. Sometimes we do our home-
>
> work at someone's house.

"To•geth•er" has three syllables as well as three vowel sounds. The writer has decided that "together" makes the first line too long and has divided "together" between the first and second syllables. "Home•work" has two syllables, and the writer has divided "homework" between its two syllables so the second line won't be too long either.

When a word has a double consonant in the middle, the word is often divided between the consonants.

> sad•dle   yel•low   ap•ple

Prefixes and suffixes are usually separate syllables.

> re•view   hope•less   dis•ap•pear

You've reached the end of a line and don't have room for the entire word. Where should you divide it? Here's a tip. In two-syllable words with a single consonant in the middle, say the first vowel sound.

If the first vowel sound is long, usually divide before the consonant in the middle.

> fa•mous   fi•nal   ro•bot

If the first vowel sound is short, usually divide after the consonant in the middle.

cab•in   pleas•ant   rob•in

Break It Up

Place hyphens between the syllables in the following words:

1. shipment

2. inside

3. terrible

4. confusion

5. yesterday

Wanted! Butcher to Cut Meat and Part Time Cashier

First, add a hyphen where it belongs. Then rewrite the help-wanted ad so the cashier is safe from harm.

Answers are on page 87.

Use a hyphen in some compound words. A **compound word** is made up of two or more smaller words. Some compound words are written as one word, such as *blackboard* and *staircase*. Others are written with hyphens between the words. You need to look the word up in a dictionary to know which is which.

mother-in-law   self-confidence   great-aunt

Use a hyphen in compound numbers and in fractions.

twenty-three   fifty-five   two-thirds   one-eighth

Use a hyphen to join the words that make up an adjective *before* a noun, as in *man-eating* tiger.

They are card-carrying members of the club.

Give him the fat-free milk.

The often-read book is missing.

Try It

Put hyphens where they belong in these sentences.
Some sentences need more than one hyphen.

1. I enjoy eating chocolate covered raisins.

2. Let's tape record the music to the show.

3. How many hard boiled eggs does the recipe call for?

4. He was an old fashioned, well to do gentleman.

5. The dropout gained self respect when he returned to school.

6. Do you want another sugar coated cookie?

7. The answer is thirty three.

8. There are twenty four students in my class.

9. The glass was two thirds full.

10. They won an all expense paid trip to Canada.

11. The well known actor is coming to town.

12. The happy go lucky boy was well liked.

13. She exercises great self control.

14. The door to door salesperson rang the doorbell.

15. Seventy six trombones led the big parade.

Answers are on page 87.

Go For It!

We went to court and saw Paul's mother in law.
Punctuate this sentence to mean the mother of Paul's wife.

Twenty odd friends came to Dan's party.
Punctuate this sentence to show that odd means "plus a few."

The sign read: DRIVE IN THEATER TURN LEFT.
Punctuate this to show that the theater is to the left.

She gave me five dollar bills.
Punctuate this sentence to show that she did not give one-dollar bills.

He needed sixty 2 inch nails.
Punctuate this sentence to show that he needed sixty nails.

He'll always get up to date cars.
Punctuate this to describe the latest cars.

Answers are on page 87.

Answers

Page 84

Break It Up
1) ship-ment; 2) in-side;
3) ter-ri-ble; 4) con-fu-sion;
5) yes-ter-day

Wanted! Part-Time Cashier and Butcher to Cut Meat

Page 85

Try It
1) I enjoy eating chocolate-covered raisins.; 2) Let's tape-record the music to the show.;
3) How many hard-boiled eggs does the recipe call for?; 4) He was an old-fashioned, well-to-do gentleman.; 5) The dropout gained self-respect when he returned to school.; 6) Do you want another sugar-coated cookie?; 7) The answer is thirty-three.; 8) There are twenty-four students in my class.; 9) The glass was two-thirds full.;
10) They won an all-expense-paid trip to Canada.; 11) The well-known actor is coming to town.; 12) The happy-go-lucky boy was well liked.; 13) She exercises great self-control.;
14) The door-to-door salesperson rang the doorbell.; 15) Seventy-six trombones led the big parade.

Page 86

Go For It!
1) We went to court and saw Paul's mother-in-law.; 2) Twenty-odd friends came to Dan's party.; 3) The sign read: DRIVE-IN THEATER. TURN LEFT.; 4) She gave me five-dollar bills.; 5) He needed sixty 2-inch nails.;
6) He'll always get up-to-date cars.

Apostrophes
It's Only Natural (Or Is It?)

Apostrophes have many functions. They can replace missing letters, show certain types of possession, and go with the plurals of letters and numbers.

Roll Call?

Each morning, the teacher calls the students names.

What's wrong with this teacher? Nothing. There's an apostrophe missing from the sentence. You need to use an **apostrophe** to show possession.

Each morning, the teacher calls the student**s'** names.

Sometimes, working with apostrophes gets tricky. How do you know when an apostrophe takes an *s* and when it doesn't? How do you know when the apostrophe goes before the *s* and when it comes after the *s?* This chapter will clear up any questions you may have.

Apostrophes Show Ownership

Use an apostrophe and *s* to form possessive nouns.

the driver**'s** seat   Mr. Jones**'s** book   Katy**'s** ring

Use an apostrophe and *s* only with the last noun in a series of possessive nouns to show joint possession.

Joe and Cathy**'s** marriage

Use an apostrophe and *s* with each noun in a series of possessive nouns to show individual possession.

Lisa**'s** and Randy**'s** clothes

Try It

Use apostrophes and an *s* to fill in the blanks in these sentences.

1. The women____ department is on the second floor.

2. Her aunt and uncle__ house is filled with paintings.

3. Tess__ homework was all correct.

4. Barbara__ and Judy____ assignments were correct.

5. The boy____ locker is locked.

6. My mom and dad____ anniversary is coming up.

7. King Arthur__ legends are still read today.

8. Tina threw the ball into the catcher__ mitt.

Answers are on page 97.

Tricks

Pronouns in Possession

Are these books yours?
No, they are Mia's books.
Nouns always need an apostrophe to become possessive, but personal pronouns do not.
Here's a list of the possessive personal pronouns:
First Person: my, mine, our, ours
Second Person: your, yours
Third Person: his, her, hers, its, their, theirs
Take a look. None of them have apostrophes.
You can remember them with help from this rhyme:
   Personal pronouns are apostrophe-less,
   Even *its* and *theirs* that end in -s.

Use an apostrophe and *s* after nonpersonal pronouns.

   everybody**'s**   somebody**'s**   anyone**'s**

Apostrophes Show Plurals

Use an apostrophe and *s* to show the plural of words, letters, numbers, and symbols.

   There are too many the**'s** in your composition.

   I have two R**'s** in my name.

   How many 7**'s** are in your telephone number?

   Don't use &**'s** in your writing; use the word *and*.

Try It

Use apostrophes and an *s* to fill in the blanks in these sentences.

1. I got three B__ and two A__ on my report card.

2. I don't want to hear any more but__ from you.

3. How many 5__ are in 5,353?

4. Two m__, two t__, and two e__ are in the word *committee*.

5. Your story is missing two ?__.

Answers are on page 97.

Apostrophes Contract

Use an apostrophe to show that one or more letters are missing in a **contraction**.

she's	(she is)
he'd	(he had, he would)
you're	(you are)
don't	(do not)
they'll	(they will)
o'clock	(of the clock)

Misfortune Cookie Humor

What two contractions can you make in the fortune below?

You are looking for a helping hand, and **you will** find it at the end of your arm.

Answer: You're, you'll

Last Chance

Write the contractions that belong in the jokes below.

Joke 1:

"_____ (that is) a strange-looking dog _____ (you have) got there."

"_____ (it is) a police dog."

"_____ (I am) surprised. He _____ (does not) look like a police dog."

"Of course not! _____ (he is) in the secret service."

Joke 2:

The TV host smiled at the grouchy game-show contestant. "Ms. Wrey," he said. "_____ (you have) just won $1,000. _____ (what is) the first thing _____ (you are) going to do when you get it?"

"Count it," she replied.

Joke 3:

"Look at those beautiful alligator shoes," Millie told Willie. "_____ (I would) sure like a pair, but _____ (they are) a fortune!"

"_____ (you have) got plenty of alligators where you live," Willie said. "Why _____ (do not) you catch one?"

The next week, Willie met Millie. "Any luck with those alligator shoes?"

"Well, I did catch an alligator," Millie said. "But he _____ (was not) wearing any shoes."

Answers are on page 97.

Soundalikes

Which word belongs in each space?

1. **their, they're**

   I know _____ waiting for me at _____ house.

2. **weed, we'd**

   ___ better get every last _____ out of this garden.

3. **he'll, heal**

   I know _____ play ball again when his legs _____.

4. **you're, your**

   _____ invited to bring _____ parents with you.

5. **aisle, I'll**

   _____ walk you down the _____.

6. **yule, you'll**

   _____ love this _____ greeting.

7. **weave, we've**

   _____ already learned how to _____.

8. **he'd, heed**

   _____ be wise to _____ my advice.

9. **there, they're**

   _____ planning to meet us _____.

10. **its, it's**

    _____ unusual for a pet to bite _____ owner.

11. **who's, whose**

    _____ going to tell me _____ book this is?

12. **their, they're**

    _____ bringing _____ folks to school.

Answers are on page 97.

Apostrophes Replace Letters and Numbers

Use an apostrophe to show that a letter or number is missing.

Rock 'n' Roll   Class of '98

Try It

Place apostrophes where they belong in these sentences.

1. Its going to be a great party.

2. Is this anyones wallet?

3. The class of 88 held the reunion at Mr. Smiths hotel.

4. You may borrow Lisas bike for a day.

5. Come up on the ships deck to see the view.

6. Dads mouth was open wide.

7. Besss jacket is missing a button.

8. There should be no *ifs, ands,* or *buts.*

9. Dont forget to dot your is and js.

10. Theyll be late again if they dont leave now.

11. Wed meet every day at three oclock.

12. Ive a new address, and Im sure you dont have it.

Answers are on page 98.

Let's Get Particular: Singular Nouns

For a *singular* noun, add an apostrophe and an *s* at the end of the noun.

Pete's computer   Murphy's doghouse

my sister's skateboard   the cat's meow

Jess's ice cream   Buzz's haircut

Jean's favorite movie   Texas's star

Slipups

Soundalikes

There eating they're lunch over their.

This sentence doesn't make sense. It has incorrectly used homophones—words that sound alike but have different spellings.

Be sure you know the meaning of homophones you use.
        there—in that place
        their—belonging to them
        they're—they are

They're eating their lunch over there.

Now that makes sense!

Let's Get Particular: Plural Nouns

For a *plural* noun that ends in *s*, just add an apostrophe.

the Garcias' house

the Meyers' car

the frogs' pond

the girls' room

For a *plural* noun that does *not* end in *s*, add an apostrophe and an *s*.

the people's election   the children's playroom

Summing It Up

Add apostrophes where they are needed to the words in the following questions. Then answer each question with a complete sentence. Be sure to add apostrophes where they are needed in your answers.

1. How many 3s are in 333.33?

2. What are the contractions for *I will, cannot,* and *it is?*

3. Wheres the principals office?

4. Do you like to listen to rock n roll music?

5. Is one of Dr. Seusss books *Green Eggs and Ham*?

6. Where are your classmates backpacks kept?

7. Can you say the ABCs backward?

8. Does the school day start at seven oclock?

9. What is your best friends address?

10. Will you be in the high school class of 16?

Answers are on page 98.

Answers

Page 89

Try It

1) The women's department is on the second floor.; 2) Her aunt and uncle's house is filled with paintings.; 3) Tess's homework was all correct.; 4) Barbara's and Judy's assignments were correct.; 5) They boy's locker is locked.; 6) My mom and dad's anniversary is coming up.; 7) King Arthur's legends are still read today.; 8) Tina threw the ball into the catcher's mitt.

Pages 91

Try It

1) I got three B's and two A's on my report card.; 2) I don't want to hear any more but's from you.; 3) How many 5's are in 5,353?; 4) Two m's, two t's, and two e's are in the word *committee*.; 5) Your story is missing two ?'s.

Page 92

Last Chance

Joke 1: That's, you've, It's, I'm, doesn't, He's

Joke 2: You've, What's, you're

Joke 3: I'd, they're, You've, don't, wasn't

Page 93

Soundalikes

1) they're, their; 2) We'd, weed; 3) he'll, heal; 4) You're, your; 5) I'll, aisle; 6) You'll, yule; 7) We've, weave; 8) He'd, heed; 9) They're, there; 10) It's, its; 11) Who's, whose; 12) They're, their

Page 94

Try It

1) It's going to be a great party.;
2) Is this anyone's wallet?; 3) The class of '88 held the reunion at Mr. Smith's hotel.; 4) You may borrow Lisa's bike for a day.;
5) Come up on the ship's deck to see the view.; 6) Dad's mouth was open wide.; 7) Bess's jacket is missing a button.; 8) There should be no *if's, and's,* or *but's.*;
9) Don't forget to dot your i's and j's.; 10) They'll be late again if they don't leave now.; 11) We'd meet every day at three o'clock.;
12) I've a new address, and I'm sure you don't have it.

Page 96

Summing It Up

Answers may vary. Sample responses are given.

1) How many 3's are in 333.33? There are five 3's in 333.33.;
2) What are the contractions for *I will, cannot,* and *it is?* The contractions are I'll, can't, and it's.; 3) Where's the principal's office? The principal's office is down the hall.; 4) Do you like to listen to rock 'n' roll music? Yes, I like to listen to rock 'n' roll music.; 5) Is one of Dr. Seuss's books *Green Eggs and Ham?* Yes, *Green Eggs and Ham* is one of Dr. Seuss's books.; 6) Where are your classmates' backpacks kept? My classmates' backpacks are kept in their lockers.;
7) Can you say the ABC's backward? Yes, I can say the ABC's backward.; 8) Does the school day start at seven o'clock? The school day starts at eight o'clock.; 9) What is your best friend's address? My best friend's address is 105 Jeffrey Street, Canton, Ohio.; 10) Will you be in the high school class of '16? No, I will not be in the high school class of '16.

Dashes, Parentheses, and Ellipses
Pardon the Interruption

Three kinds of punctuation marks either add to or take information from sentences. In the pages that follow, you'll learn how to use them.

When to Use the Dash (—)

Read the following two questions aloud.

Where's the book I loaned you in the park?

Where's the book I loaned you—in the park?

Did you pause when you came to the **dash** (—) in the second sentence? Good. Which of the answers below matches the question with the dash?

Yes, it is, but I'll go right back and find it.

It's here in my desk.

The first one. That's because the dash was used to set off a final summary, *in the park.*

Use a pair of dashes to show a sudden break in a sentence, such as a change in thought or direction.

The kids—in case you hadn't noticed—act like animals at school.

When are you going—not that I care—to the zoo?

Chapter Eight

Use a dash to show an interrupted or unfinished statement.

Hi! Come in—excuse me, I'm on the phone.

JUST A SHORT DASH

Harry S. Truman (1884–1972)

Did you notice the short dash between President Truman's birth year and the year he died? It's not as long as a regular dash (—) or as short as a hyphen (-).

This short dash is used between numbers to mean *through* or *between*. Harry Truman lived *between* 1884 and 1972.

Read pages 25–30.

Here, the short dash means through. Read pages 25 *through* 30.

Remember, you need just a short dash between numbers.

Try It

Put dashes in the following sentences where they are needed.

1. I read on pages 5 19 that people from all over the world especially Germany and Ireland came to the United States between 1880 and 1900.

2. Here's the bus oh, no, where did I put my homework?

Answers are on page 106.

When to Use Parentheses

Use **parentheses** ( ) to set off added information that is contained in the sentence. Use parentheses sparingly. Do not use them in formal writing, except for the years of a person's life.

I'm using the chart (figure 2) on page 42.

Alice loves to skate (she always has).

Punctuation that belongs to the added information goes *inside* the parentheses. Punctuation that belongs to the whole sentence goes *outside* the parentheses.

Mom drove us to school (Dad had said, "I can't").

Use parentheses for the years of a person's life.

Thomas Jefferson (1743–1826) was the third president of the United States.

Try It

Put parentheses where they belong in the following sentences.

1. After school, we ate and played basketball Joe's favorite game.

2. I'm counting the days to the holiday I can hardly wait, which is not for another week.

3. Was Tommy watching TV he had promised not to?

4. I'm reading about Wolfgang Mozart 1756–1791.

5. Chocolate cake it's Mom's preferred dessert will be served.

Answers are on page 106.

When to Use Ellipses . . .

Use an **ellipsis** (. . .) to show that one or more words have been left out of a quotation.

Complete Quote:

"I think that the game begins at four o'clock, so if we want good seats we'll have to get there by 3:30 P.M."

Shortened Quote:

". . . the game begins at four o'clock . . . we'll have to get there by 3:30 P.M."

Use an ellipsis to show a pause in dialogue or at the end where dialogue trails off. If the ellipsis is at the end of a sentence, use *four* periods.

"I'm ... speechless," he said.

"I'm speechless ... ," he said.

"I'm speechless...."

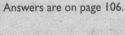

Try It

Add ellipses where they are needed in these sentences.

1. "in the house, where we found it" is a statement from the book.

2. "It's it's so sudden," Sue said when Bob proposed.

3. I've run out of energy and tissues.

Answers are on page 106.

In a Fix?

What's wrong with the sentences below? Fix them with apostrophes, hyphens, dashes, and parentheses.

Thirty three people were at my parents anniversary party. The cake three large layers was beautiful. It had the couples marriage dates 1990 2003 written in chocolate icing.

Answers are on page 106.

Make Your Mark

Here's your chance to review some of the material from the last few chapters: apostrophes, hyphens, dashes, and parentheses.

Where are the *apostrophes* needed in the following sentences?

1. What do the 3s mean in this board game?

2. Dont forget there are four ss and two ps in *Mississippi*.

3. It doesnt have to be that difficult.

4. Mrs. Rosss paper is due tomorrow.

5. I had to pick up the childrens toys.

6. Where are Sarahs shoes?

7. Betty and Anns sister look alike.

8. Today Ill sit on Freds throne.

9. Marks and Bills teachers gave the same test.

10. We enjoy the music from Buzzs collection.

Answers are on page 106.

Where are the *hyphens, dashes,* and *parentheses* needed in the following sentences?

1. Roger ate all the sugar coated cookies.

2. Pete and Paul are very close most twins are.

3. Charles Lindbergh 1902 1974 was a flying pioneer.

4. The mayor the one we voted for presented the award.

5. I like sleeping on a king size bed.

6. Colonists stuffed their beds with whatever they could find straw, cornhusks, wood chips.

7. The cake is one third vanilla and two thirds chocolate.

8. The teenagers Margie and Kim volunteered.

9. She was a well respected authority on planets.

10. I'm self conscious about my freckles.

Answers are on page 106.

Answers

Page 100

Try It

1) I read on pages 5–19 that people from all over the world—especially Germany and Ireland—came to the United States between 1880 and 1900.; 2) Here's the bus—oh, no, where did I put my homework?

Page 102

Try It

1) After school, we ate and played basketball (Joe's favorite game).; 2) I'm counting the days to the holiday (I can hardly wait), which is not for another week.; 3) Was Tommy watching TV (he had promised not to)?; 4) I'm reading about Wolfgang Mozart (1756–1791).; 5) Chocolate cake (it's Mom's preferred dessert) will be served.

Page 103

Try It

1) " . . . in the house, where we found it" is a statement from the book.; 2) "It's . . . it's so sudden," Sue said when Bob proposed.; 3) I've run out of energy . . . and tissues.

Page 104

In a Fix?

Thirty-three people were at my parents' anniversary party. The cake (three large layers) was beautiful. It had the couple's marriage dates (1990–2003) written in chocolate icing.

Pages 104–105

Make Your Mark

1) 3's; 2) Don't, s's, p's; 3) doesn't; 4) Ross's; 5) children's; 6) Sarah's; 7) Ann's; 8) I'll, Fred's; 9) Mark's, Bill's; 10) Buzz's

(second set of questions)

1) Roger ate all the sugar-coated cookies.; 2) Pete and Paul are very close—most twins are. *or* Pete and Paul are very close (most twins are).; 3) Charles Lindbergh (1902–1974) was a flying pioneer.; 4) The mayor (the one we voted for) presented the award.; 5) I like sleeping on a king-size bed.; 6) Colonists stuffed their beds with whatever they could find—straw, corn-husks, wood chips.; 7) The cake is one-third vanilla and two-thirds chocolate.; 8) The teenagers—Margie and Kim—volunteered.; 9) She was a well-respected authority on planets.; 10) I'm self-conscious about my freckles.

Capitalization
A Capital Idea!

Do you ever have questions about capitalization when you write? You'll find all you need to know about capitalization in this chapter.

Capital Letters Count

What's the difference between boy scouts and Boy Scouts? Is it just the capital letters? Without the capital letters, you couldn't tell the difference between boys who get information and a well-known organization.

Take the Challenge!

1. To which sentence might a woman answer "thank you"?

a. Here's your dollar, Bill.
b. Here's your dollar bill.

2. Which sentence suggests that someone has a flat tire?

a. I need the car jack.
b. I need the car, Jack.

Answers: 1.b. Here's your dollar bill.
2.a. I need the car jack.

Here's another example: What's the difference between *red cross* and *Red Cross*? In which case is the color of the cross important? In which case do the words name an organization that helps people?

Finally, what's the difference between *green berets* and *Green Berets*? Which means green hats? Which is a military group?

These examples tell something important about capital letters: **A word that begins with a capital letter is special in some way.**

When to Use Capital Letters

> *He danced with Joy.*
>
> *He danced with joy.*

Both sentences have the same words, but they have different meanings. Which sentence matches the picture?

Use a capital letter to show where a sentence begins.

> **C**ome to my party tomorrow. **W**e will have a good time.
>
> **L**et's go to the movies. **T**he movie starts at three o'clock.

Use the word *I* when you talk about yourself. The word *I* is always spelled capital *I*.

> You and **I** are best friends. Oh, **I** am glad **I** know you.

Use capital letters to begin a person's name.

> **George Washington**   **Halle Berry**   **Tiger Woods**

Try It

How would you correct these sentences?

1. i like to read books about abraham lincoln.

   _____.

2. robert frost wrote many poems.

   _____.

3. my friend and i were born on the same day.

   _____.

4. mr. and mrs. block took us to see a movie.

   _____.

Answers are on page 131.

More about Capital Letters

Capitalize words such as *Mom* and *Dad* when they are used as names.

> When I'm hungry, **D**ad fixes me a snack.

> (In this case, *Dad* is used as a name.)

> **A**unt **M**ay wrote me a letter.

> (In this case, the word *aunt* is used as part of a name.)

But remember: You do not need to capitalize a family name if it comes after a word like *my, our* (or any other possessive pronoun), or even *the!*

My mom is the best mom in the world!

Our aunt and uncle will be visiting us.

The dad took his kids to the park.

Capitalize the first word in a line of poetry.

Roses are red,

Violets are blue,

Sugar is sweet,

And so are you.

Capitalize the first word in each sentence.

The name Jeep came from the abbreviation used in the army for the "General Purpose" vehicle, GP.

Baby sea horses hatch inside a pocket on their father's belly.

A grown-up flounder has both eyes on one side of its head.

Some monarch butterflies travel more than 2,000 miles south for the winter.

Most bats sleep hanging upside down.

Capitalize the first word in a sentence when someone is talking.

"**A** rolling stone gathers no moss," said Grandpa.

Who said, "**A** bird in the hand is worth two in the bush"?

"**E**very day," she explained, "he runs two miles." ("Every" is the beginning of the sentence, not "he.")

"That's true," he said. "**S**he goes bike riding." ("She" is the beginning of the second sentence.)

Town Party

Guest List:

Mayor Brian McMahon
Karen Adams
Jamal Lewis
Mr. Roy Street
Ms. Donna H. Hughes
Mrs. Joy Frankel
Dr. Ben J. Newman
Capt. Frank Todd
Pres. Gloria Rose
PTA Chair Stan Back

You are cordially invited to the 50th anniversary of Pleasant Valley

Reasons why the letters in the Town-Party Guest List are capitalized

- All **first and last names** begin with a capital letter.
- An **initial** in a name is capitalized.
- A **title** is capitalized when it is used with a name.

- Sometimes titles are abbreviated, or made shorter, as in the following examples:

Mr. for a man
Ms. for any woman
Mrs. for a married woman
Dr. for a doctor
Capt. for a captain, as in the police force
Pres. for the president of a club or organization

Proper Nouns

A **proper noun** names a particular person, place, or thing.
Proper nouns always begin with capital letters.

<u>Cities</u>	<u>Streets and Roads</u>
Los Angeles	Main Street
New York	Pelham Parkway
Chicago	Avenue of the Americas

<u>States</u>	<u>Buildings, Bridges, and Monuments</u>
Texas	
California	George Washington Bridge
Virginia	Statue of Liberty
Illinois	Empire State Building

<u>Countries</u>	<u>Public Places</u>
France	Washington Square Park
Thailand	Pleasant Valley Mall
Egypt	Houston City Hall

<u>Continents</u>	<u>Names of Regions</u>
South America	the Middle East
Asia	the Southwest
Australia	Central Asia

<u>Bodies of Water</u>	<u>Planets and Heavenly Bodies</u>
Atlantic Ocean	Milky Way Galaxy
Mississippi River	Mars
Lake Placid	Earth

<u>Landforms</u>
Grand Canyon
Gobi Desert
Rocky Mountains

Try It

Correct these sentences.

1. michael jordan was a great basketball player.

_____

2. i saw him play in madison square garden.

_____

3. madison square garden is in new york city.

_____

4. he also played for the wizards.

_____

5. michael jordan went to the university of north carolina.

_____

6. he majored in math.

_____

7. michael's favorite saying is "keep your eye on the ball."

_____

Answers are on page 131.

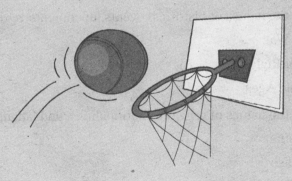

The Name Game

There are more rules for
capitalization, but don't give up
now. Keep going. There's a
surprise at the end of this chapter.

Capitalize the names of people
and the initials that stand for those names.

> **Martin Luther King, Jr.**

> **M. E. Kerr**

Capitalize names of organizations, businesses, teams, and
political groups.

> **Girl Scouts of America**

> **Democratic Party**

> **L.A. Lakers**

Capitalize abbreviations of titles and organizations.

> **NBA** (National Basketball Association)

> **PTA** (Parent-Teacher Association)

> **Ph.D.** (Doctor of Philosophy)

Capitalize the names of historical events, documents, and times.

> **Civil War**

> **Bill of Rights**

> **Middle Ages**

Capitalize the names of religions, nationalities, and languages.

> **Christian**

> **Swedish**

> **Spanish**

Go for It!

See if you can correct these sentences.
(Hint: There are 20 letters that need to be capitalized.)

1. My teacher graduated from college with an m.a. degree
   in english.

   _____.

2. Abraham lincoln was president during the civil war.

   _____.

3. Martin Luther King, jr., led the March on washington.

   _____.

4. The republicans will choose their party leader.

   _____.

5. I am learning french in school.

   _____.

6. My friend celebrates hindu holidays.

   _____.

7. The egyptian pharaohs were very powerful.

   _____.

8. The miami heat is her favorite basketball team.

   _____.

9. nasa will launch another spacecraft.

   _____.

10. Which men signed the declaration of independence?

   _____.

Answers are on page 131.

Take a Test

Now it's time to practice! Write the answer to each question below. As you do, you'll be practicing the rules for correct capitalization. Write in complete sentences.

What is the name of a famous historical document?

_____.

Who is your favorite male movie star?

_____.

Who is your favorite female singer?

_____.

What nationalities are you?

_____.

What month is it?

_____.

What is the name of your favorite sports team?

_____.

What are the names of two continents?

_____.

What is the name of a body of water?

_____.

What state would you like to visit?

_____.

What is a famous tourist spot?

_____.

Answers will vary.

Time for a Holiday (well, almost)

We've covered a lot of ground, but you don't have to remember everything you read right away. You can always come back to this chapter when you are unsure when to capitalize. The more you practice correct capitalization, the sooner you'll know what to do without giving it a second thought.

Capitalize the days of the week.

Friday

Sunday

Capitalize the months of the year.

January

March

Capitalize holidays.

Passover

Christmas

Capitalize the names of ships, trains, planes, and spacecraft.

Titanic

Metro **N**orth

Concorde

Apollo 11

Capitalize the names of product brands, awards, and numbered educational courses.

Cheerios

Grammy **A**ward

History 2

Do NOT capitalize the names of the seasons (winter, spring, summer, fall) **or directions** (north, south, east, west)

Try It

Correct these sentences.

1. If you liked Shakespeare, you'll want to read another shakespearean play.

   _____

2. Former President Carter received the nobel peace prize.

   _____

3. We traveled through europe on the orient express.

   _____

4. I borrowed lisa's sneakers.

   _____

5. i will attend john f. kennedy junior high school in the fall.

   _____

6. We have a quiz every friday.

   _____

7. My birthday is may 13.

   _____

8. School will be closed for easter.

   _____

9. I want to visit south carolina next year.

   _____

10. new year's day falls on january 1.

    _____

Answers are on page 131.

Time Out!

You deserve a break. Read the joke below. It contains 12 mistakes in capitalization. How many can you find?

On monday, the teacher, mrs. lake, found a careless mistake in noah way's english paper. Mrs. lake said, "you misspelled the word *february*."

Noah Way replied, "i'll fix it." He added, "i'll even do another assignment for you."

"All right," mrs. Lake replied. "Write a long sentence."

Noah wrote only three words. But he got an A. What was his long sentence?

Answers are on page 131.

FOR THE PUN OF IT

Here are some riddles for you to enjoy. As you read, circle the letters that should be capitalized.

1. What did ben franklin say when he discovered electricity?
   Nothing. He was too shocked.

2. What time is it when a knight from the dark ages looks at his belly button?
   It is the middle of the night (knight).

3. How can you learn geography at airports?
   You can find the Great plains (planes) there.

4. Why are saturday and sunday the strongest days?
   Because monday through friday are weak days (weekdays).

5. Which country serves the most fried foods?
   greece (grease).

6. Why did The Great santini cancel his magic show when he lost his rabbit?
   He didn't have any more hare restorer (hair restorer).

7. How do you know when you've missed the orient express?
You can see its tracks.

8. What is muhammad ali's favorite drink?
Punch.

9. What kind of music did the neanderthal have 10,000 years ago?
Rock.

10. Why do animals like to watch *jeopardy*?
Because it's a game show.

11. Why didn't frosty the snowman ask someone to dance?
He had cold feet.

12. What do gymnasts do on valentine's day?
They fall head over heels in love.

13. Why was the abominable snowman a snob?
He gave everyone the cold shoulder.

14. Why was robin hood of sherwood forest arrested?
He was shooting the breeze.

Answers are on pages 131–132.

> **Remember to capitalize adjectives made from proper nouns.**
>
> **Proper noun:** Italy
>
> **Proper adjective:** Italian

Great Works

Capitalize the first word, last word, and all other words in titles except for conjunctions (and, but, or), articles (the, a, an), and prepositions (from, for, by, away, below, to, etc).

Books	*Harry Potter and the Sorcerer's Stone*
Magazines	*National Geographic for Kids*
Newspapers	*The New York Times*
Short stories	"The Monkey's Paw"
Movies	*Star Wars*
Plays	*Julius Caesar*
TV shows	*Law and Order*
Musical works	the opera *Madame Butterfly*
	the song "The Star-Spangled Banner"
Works of art	the painting "Sunflowers"

Try It

Correct these sentences.

1. My favorite TV show is *friends*.

   _____.

2. When I visit chicago, I read the *chicago tribune*.

   _____.

3. The magazine I enjoy the most is *kids discover*.

   _____.

4. Leonardo da Vinci's painting "Mona lisa" is known around
   the world.

   _____.

5. After I watched the world Series, I rented the movie
   The rookie.

   _____.

6. I like detectives and mysteries. that is why i read all the
   Nate the great books.

   _____.

7. We are putting on scenes from *west side story*.

   _____.

8. When I finish my homework, I like to watch
   Wheel of fortune.

   _____.

9. We are learning the words to "Can you Feel the love
   Tonight?" from *The lion king*.

   _____.

10. I am writing a story entitled "my secret life."

   _____.

Answers are on page 132.

Write Away!

You need to know the rules for capitalization when you write letters.

Capitalize the words in the greeting of a letter.

Dear John,   **Dear Sir or Madam:**

Capitalize only the first word in the closing.

Sincerely yours,   **Y**our friend,

Write Again!

Use capitals for the first letter in abbreviations in an address (capitalize both letters in postal abbreviations for states).

Juana **P**erez
3565 **N.** Main **St.**
Chicago, **IL** 60650

Dear Juana,

Hello from Nevada. I just saw Hoover Dam. It's huge! I'll show you the pictures when I get back.

Your friend,

Rita

Shortcuts

Here are some common abbreviations you can use when you are addressing letters and postcards. For these abbreviations, begin with a capital letter and end with a period.

For Words Used in Addresses

Apt.	Apartment	**N.**	North
Ave.	Avenue	**Pkwy.**	Parkway
Blvd.	Boulevard	**Pl.**	Place
Ct.	Court	**Rd.**	Road
Dr.	Drive	**S.**	South
E.	East	**Sq.**	Square
Hwy.	Highway	**St.**	Street
Ln.	Lane	**W.**	West

NETIQUETTE:

Do you know it's considered rude to use all capital letters online? It's the same thing as SHOUTING, and no one likes to be yelled at!

Baker's Dozen

Can you find 13 words whose first letter should be capitalized?

dear Eileen,

I miss you already. I think boston is nice, but i still miss california. My new school is called John Jay junior high. The principal's name is dr. Lewis.

I made a new friend at lunch yesterday. her name is janet jones. We have the same birthday. She was born on tuesday, december 3—just like me!

Got to go. Write back soon.

your friend,

Ima

Address the Envelope

Can you find the 11 letters that need to be capitalized on the envelope?

Ima nut
2018 cedar lane
Brooklyn, ny 11202

eileen dover
100 mountaintop avenue
san francisco, CA 94301

Tip
Don't use abbreviations in formal writing. Spell out names of states, countries, months, days, and units of measure.

Answers are on page 132.

Let's Recap

Are you are ready to take this capital challenge?

Write a proper noun for each category.

city _____

school _____

holiday _____

park _____

person _____

Fill in the missing days of the week.

Monday, _____, Wednesday,

Thursday, _____, Saturday, _____

Answers are on page 132.

Complete each sentence by adding a title.

My favorite song is _____.

My favorite TV show is _____.

My favorite movie is _____.

Write the answers to these questions.

What is today's date? _____

In what month were you born? _____

What is your favorite time of year? _____

What day of the week is it? _____

What is the title of the last
book you read? _____

Write the name of a place next to each category.

country _____

planet _____

state _____

ocean _____

street _____

When the word "Capitol" refers to a specific building,
capitalize the "C" in Capitol. When the word "capital"
refers to a city that is the seat of government, don't
capitalize the "c" in capital.

Slipups

French or french fries?
Do not capitalize the "f" in the word "french" when referring to "french fries."

Some nouns and adjectives come from proper nouns, but they are not capitalized.

We used plaster of paris to make a model of the Arc de Triomphe in Paris.

She mailed that manila envelope to Manila.

Remember, if a word that comes from a proper noun has a common, everyday meaning, do not capitalize it.

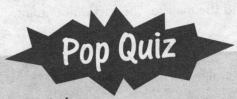

Pop Quiz

What a Capital Idea!

You can do this alone (maybe you'd like to time yourself) or with a friend. Be sure to use a separate piece of paper so you can try this one again and again.

Correct one of the examples in each pair.

Statue of Liberty	Grant's tomb
Colorado River	lake mead
yellowstone national park	Lincoln Memorial

Correct the titles and names.

dr. frankenstein

mrs. Doubtfire

Marcus Welby, m.d.

pres. bush

Correct the errors in these sentences.

1. Labor day is always the first Monday in september.

2. My favorite subjects are english and math.

3. I am in the sixth grade at Jefferson middle school.

4. My great-uncle served in world war II.

5. I searched the map for the rocky mountains.

6. texas is near the gulf of mexico.

7. Would you like a spanish omelette?

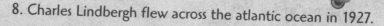

8. Charles Lindbergh flew across the atlantic ocean in 1927.

9. Are Alaska and hawaii the two newest states?

10. The declaration of independence involved 13 colonies.

Answers are on page 132.

CONGRATULATIONS! YOU'VE MADE IT TO
THE END OF THIS CHAPTER—THE LONGEST
CHAPTER IN THE WHOLE BOOK.
GIVE YOURSELF A HAND.

Answers

Page 109

Try It
1) I like to read books about Abraham Lincoln.; 2) Robert Frost wrote many poems.; 3) My friend and I were born on the same day.; 4) Mr. and Mrs. Block took us to see a movie.

Page 113

Try It
1) Michael Jordan was a great basketball player.; 2) I saw him play in Madison Square Garden.; 3) Madison Square Garden is in New York City.; 4) He also played for the Wizards.; 5) Michael Jordan went to the University of North Carolina.; 6) He majored in math.; 7) Michael's favorite saying is "Keep your eye on the ball."

Page 115

Go for It!
1) M.A., English; 2) Lincoln, Civil War; 3) Jr., Washington; 4) Republicans; 5) French; 6) Hindu; 7) Egyptian; 8) Miami, Heat; 9) NASA; 10) Declaration, Independence

Page 118

Try It
1) If you liked Shakespeare, you'll want to read another Shakespearean play.; 2) Former President Carter received the Nobel Peace Prize.; 3) We traveled through Europe on the Orient Express.; 4) I borrowed Lisa's sneakers.; 5) I will attend John F. Kennedy Junior High School in the fall.; 6) We have a quiz every Friday.; 7) My birthday is May 13.; 8) School will be closed for Easter.; 9) I want to visit South Carolina next year.; 10) New Year's Day falls on January 1.

Page 119

Time Out!
(12 errors in order)
Monday, Mrs., Lake, Noah, Way's, English, Lake, You, February, I'll, I'll, Mrs.
(Answer: Life in Prison)

Pages 120-121

For the Pun of It
1) Ben Franklin; 2) Dark Ages; 3) Plains; 4) Saturday, Sunday,

Monday, Friday; 5) Greece;
6) Santini; 7) Orient Express;
8) Muhammad Ali's; 9) Neanderthal;
10) *Jeopardy;* 11) Frosty,
Snowman; 12) Valentine's Day;
13) Abominable Snowman;
14) Robin Hood, Sherwood Forest

Page 123

Try It
1) *Friends;* 2) Chicago, *Chicago
Tribune;* 3) *Kids Discover;*
4) "Lisa"; 5) World, *Rookie;*
6) That, I, *Great;* 7) *West Side
Story;* 8) *Fortune;* 9) "You,"
"Love," *Lion King;* 10) "My
Secret Life"

Page 126

Baker's Dozen
Dear Eileen,

I miss you already. I think
Boston is nice, but I still miss
California. My new school is
called John Jay Junior High. The
principal's name is Dr. Lewis.

I made a new friend at lunch
yesterday. Her name is Janet
Jones. We have the same
birthday. She was born on
Tuesday, December 3—just
like me!

Got to go. Write back soon.
Your friend,
Ima

Address the Envelope
Ima Nut
2018 Cedar Lane
Brooklyn, NY 11202

Eileen Dover
100 Mountaintop Avenue
San Francisco, CA 94301

Page 127

Let's Recap
**Answers will vary except for
days of the week:**
Tuesday; Friday; Sunday

Pages 129–130

Pop Quiz
**Correct one of the examples in
each pair.**

Grant's Tomb; Lake Mead;
Yellowstone National Park

Correct the titles and names.

Dr. Frankenstein; Mrs. Doubtfire;
Marcus Welby, M.D.; Pres. Bush

**Correct the errors in these
sentences.**
1) Day, September; 2) English;
3) Middle School; 4) World War;
5) Rocky Mountains; 6) Texas,
Gulf, Mexico; 7) Spanish;
8) Atlantic Ocean; 9) Hawaii;
10) Declaration, Independence

Numbers, Proofreading Symbols, and Review
On Your Mark, Get Set, Go!

This chapter *marks* the end of the book. In it, you'll find bits and pieces of information that you'll need to know when you write. You'll also learn important proofreading symbols to help you when you make corrections. But that's not all. There are fun games, too!

We've Got Your Number!

Here are a few details you should know about writing numbers. If two numbers are close together, spell out the first one and use digits for the other one.

> I read **three 50**-page books.

> Rachel carried **two 10**-pound balls to the field.

Always spell out a number that begins a sentence.

> **One hundred twenty-five** parents attended the school meeting.

> **Four** is my favorite number.

Don't begin a sentence with a year.

> I was born in **1997.**

> *not* **1997** was when I was born.

Chapter Ten

Spell out the time when you use the word *o'clock*. Use numerals when the time is followed by A.M. and P.M. or is used alone as an exact time.

> Let's meet at **three o'clock**.

> Let's schedule the meeting for **4:00 P.M.**

> We took the **3:20** train. It arrived at **3:45**.

Fractions

Spell out fractions for common fractions, but use numerals for complicated fractions.

> **two-thirds** of the class

> $^{29}/_{32}$ an inch

Hyphenate word fractions only when they're used as adjectives but not when they are nouns.

> a **three-fourths** majority

> **one half** of the population

When possible, change fractions to decimals.

> **2.5** million, *not* $2^{1}/_{2}$ million

Know Your Numbers

Correct the numbers in these sentences.

1. 13 more days is a long time to wait for a birthday present.

2. Shannon has 6 3-inch caterpillars in her jar.

3. A $\frac{1}{4}$ slice of the pie was on the table.

4. Did you come to school at 9 thirty-two in the morning?

5. "5 of your friends can come," my mom told me.

6. I go to bed at 10 o'clock.

7. Henry went to the store and bought 8 120-card baseball sets.

Answers are on page 143.

Proofreading

When you rewrite your work or check the work of others, it's helpful to use **proofreading symbols.** As you make corrections, write the symbols to show exactly the kinds of changes that are needed.

Proofreading Symbols
Here are the most common proofreading symbols.

⊙ _____ add a period

/∧ _____ add a space

cap or **[three lines]** _____ capitalization

l.c. or **[slash through the letter]** _____ use a lowercase (not capital) letter

⌀ **[paragraph symbol]** _____ new paragraph

? _____ unclear; rewrite

∧ _____ add something

sp. _____ correct spelling

∽ **[tr]** _____ change order of words

⚲ **[delete]** _____ take something out

◡ _____ close up space

⌐ _____ break sentence or word

= /∧ _____ add a hyphen

Try It

Use proofreading symbols to correct the ten errors in this letter.

Dear Diary,

Mom and I went shopping this afternoon we picked up a lot of stuff for my sleep over. I can't wait until friday! We bought pizza dough, cheese, and sauce. Were going to make our own pizza! Guess what we're doing for desert. We bought cake and ice cream. My Mom even let me get get snacks for when we watch the movie.

Answers are on page 143.

Trick

Sounding Like *a* . . .

Proofread the following sentence. Can you find the spelling error?

My nieghbor grew a pumpkin that weighed 100 pounds.

You probably know the memory trick for spelling words like *receive:*

i before *e* except after *c.*

Did you know the memory trick has another line?

. . . and when sounding like *a* as in *neighbor* and *weigh.*

That's right, *neighbor* is misspelled in the sentence. Remember the whole rhyme. It can help you proofread for spelling.

Review Checklist

Use this checklist when you edit and proofread your schoolwork.

End Marks

___Did I end all my sentences with either a period, a question mark, or an exclamation point?

___Did I use the appropriate end punctuation mark for each sentence?

___Did I make sure that I did not use too many exclamation points?

Commas

___Did I use commas to separate words and phrases in a series?

___Did I use a comma to separate items in dates and addresses?

___Did I use commas when addressing people?

___Did I use commas after words such as *however, therefore,* and *of course?*

___Did I use a comma to set off the words of a speaker from the rest of the sentence?

___Did I use a comma when a conjunction such as *and, but,* and *or* joins two independent clauses?

___Did I use commas to set off introductory phrases or clauses, such as *After a long day, I slept like a log?*

___Did I use a comma for large numbers such as *1,000* and *1,000,000?*

___Did I use commas with words that explain nouns, as in *My friend, a swimmer, wins many meets?*

___Did I use a comma to separate a short exclamation from the rest of the sentence?

Quotation Marks

___Did I use quotation marks before and after spoken words?

___Did I put periods and commas inside the quotation marks if they belong with the quote?

___Did I put punctuation marks outside the quotation marks if they belong with the whole sentence?

Colon

____Did I use a colon to introduce a list, a quote, or a summary?

____Did I use a colon to separate the minutes and hours when writing the time?

Semicolon

____Did I use a semicolon to join two independent clauses that may each stand alone?

____Did I use a semicolon to separate a series of phrases that already have commas?

Hyphens

____Did I use a hyphen to divide a word at the end of a line?

____Did I use a hyphen to join two or more words that make an adjective before a noun?

Apostrophes

____Did I use an apostrophe in each contraction?

____Did I use an apostrophe to show plurals?

____Did I use an apostrophe and s with singular nouns and nouns that end in s or z?

____Did I use an apostrophe for plural nouns ending in s?

____When two or more nouns share possession, did I put an apostrophe after the last noun?

Parentheses

____Did I use parentheses to add information?

____Did I use parentheses for the years of a person's life?

Dashes and Ellipses

____Did I use a dash to show a sudden break in a sentence?

____Did I use an ellipsis to show that one or more words were omitted from a quote?

____Did I use an ellipsis to show a pause in dialogue or where dialogue trails off?

Capitalization

____Did I begin each sentence with a capital letter?

____Did I capitalize nouns that name particular people, places, things, and ideas?

____Did I always capitalize "I"?

Letter Writing

____Did I address the envelope correctly?

____Did I include my return address?

____Did I use a comma after the greeting of a friendly letter and a colon after the greeting of a business letter?

____Did I capitalize the first word of the closing and put a comma at the end of the closing?

Writing Titles

____Did I use italics or underlining to set off the titles of books, newspapers, plays, TV shows, magazines, movies, and CDs?

____Did I use quotation marks to set off the titles of poems, short stories, magazine articles, songs, essays, and chapters?

"Extras"

___Did I use italics or underlining to show emphasis in a sentence?

That's one *huge* tree!

___Did I put quotation marks around special words in a sentence?

She came up with a "reason," but it was really lame.

___Did I use a period with abbreviations, such as Dr. and P.M.?

The Last Laugh

Riddles can make you laugh. They can also help you review some of the punctuation skills you've learned in this book. The part of each riddle that has to do with punctuation appears in *bold*. For each riddle, think of the rule it demonstrates. The first one is done for you.

1. What did the pony whisper?
   I'm a little hoarse.
   (In the contraction, an apostrophe takes the place of the letter *a* in the word *am*.)

2. What do you call a chicken that thinks it is Superman?
   Cluck Kent.

3. Why isn't your nose 12-**in.** long?
   *Because then your 12-**in.** nose would be a foot.*

4. What did the sock say to the foot?
   You're putting me on.

Answers are on page 143.

Summing It Up

Correct the following sentences with the proper punctuation and capitalization.

1. check that all sentences begin with a capital letter and that proper nouns, like sunday, do too. Be sure Capital letters are not used where they are not needed.

2. Take out, punctuation that does not belong add punctuation where it is needed

3. Is everything speled correctly? If not, fix the spelling.

4. Are words in the order proper? Change their order if necessary.

5. Remember that commas separate phrases in a series are placed after letter greetings and set off introductory phrases.

6. Colons are used in these ways to separate hours and minutes in time references such as 10 15 and as introductions to lists and quotations.

7. Dashes are used to signal a sudden change you know what I mean in thought.

8. How did you do. No mistakes? Congratulations you've finished the book.

Answers are on page 143.

Answers

Page 135

Know Your Numbers
1) Thirteen; 2) six; 3) one-fourths;
4) 9:32; 5) "Five"; 6) ten; 7) eight

Page 136

Try It

Dear Diary,
Mom and I went shopping this
afternoon, we picked up a lot
of stuff for my sleep over. I
can't wait until friday! We
bought pizza dough, cheese,
and sauce. We're going to
make our own pizza! Guess
what we're doing for desert.
We bought cake and ice
cream. My Mom even let me
get get snacks for when we
watch the movie.

Page 141

The Last Laugh
(Answers will vary, but here are
suggested answers.)
1) In the contraction, an apostrophe takes the place of the
letter a in the word am.; 2) Capitalize the proper nouns for the
name Cluck Kent.; 3) Put a
period after the abbreviation for
inch ("in.").; 4) In the contraction,
an apostrophe takes the place of
the letter a in the word are.

Page 142

Summing It Up
1) Check that all sentences begin
with a capital letter and that
proper nouns, like Sunday, do
too. Be sure capital letters are
not used where they are not
needed.; 2) Take out punctuation
that does not belong; add
punctuation where it is needed.;
4) Is everything spelled
correctly? If not, fix the spelling.;
5) Are words in the proper order?
Change their order if necessary.;
6) Remember that commas
separate phrases in a series, are
placed after letter greetings, and
set off introductory phrases.;
6) Colons are used in these
ways: to separate hours and
minutes in time references such
as 10:15 and as introductions to
lists and quotations.; 7) Dashes
are used to signal a sudden
change—you know what I
mean—in thought.; 8) How did
you do? No mistakes?
Congratulations! You've finished
the book.

Index